Open Networked "i-Learning"

Gianluca Elia • Antonella Poce

Editors

Open Networked "i-Learning"

Models and Cases of "Next-Gen" Learning

Foreword by Aldo Romano

 Springer

Editors
Gianluca Elia
University of Salento
Department of Innovation Engineering
Euro-Mediterranean Incubator
Via per Monteroni s.n.
73100 Lecce
Campus Ecotekne
Italy
gianluca.elia@unisalento.it

Antonella Poce
Università Roma Tre
Department for Educational Design
Via della Madonna dei Monti 40
00184 Roma
Italy
poce@uniroma3.it

ISBN 978-1-4899-9707-4   ISBN 978-1-4419-6854-8 (eBook)
DOI 10.1007/978-1-4419-6854-8
Springer New York Dordrecht Heidelberg London

Printed on acid-free paper

Springer is part of Springer Science+Business Media (www.springer.com)

To my parents, Marco and Ebe,
Who made possible the learning
experience which is my life

(Gianluca Elia)

To Fabrizio and Alessandro

(Antonella Poce)

Foreword

In current global business scenario, productivity and competitiveness are increasingly dependent on the capability and efficiency of organizations to generate, process and apply knowledge at intra- and inter-organizational level. This implies that, to obtain and sustain competitive advantage, organizations have to learn better and faster than their competitors. So, learning becomes the core process of the organization, a powerful "weapon" to face the rapid and unpredictable changes within hypercompetitive markets. Actually, some on field researches identified the "learning organization" model as a value creating configuration (in terms of sales per employees, revenue growth and net income growth). Today, Human Capital proves to be fundamental for innovation and business performance, more than the role played by Financial and Physical Capital.

At the same time, the tremendous development of the ICT (Information and Communication Technologies) is generating an extraordinary and pervasive impact on social and business relationships, accelerating processes and enhancing significantly the obsolescence rate of products and services.

Framed into this mindset, human resource can be conceived as a particular kind of "extended-product", with a higher level of complexity for its hybrid nature due to the influence of services, and its strong and multifaceted characteristics embracing different disciplines, fields and contexts (pedagogy, psychology, economy, innovation, technology, organization, etc.). Thus, as a product, also the human resource with its knowledge, skills and competencies is subjected to the rapid obsolescence phenomenon. Nowadays, its life cycle is becoming shorter and narrower and, since we live in a knowledge-based economy, it is emerging a sense of "urgency" in fulfilling the knowledge and competency gaps.

Trying to stop or ignore the resulting complex scenario is practically impossible; pointing out few and simple rules to manage the complexity and to create value from it, it is a must to be pursued!

The first driving simple rule to take in high consideration is represented by the *lifelong learning* paradigm. This drives human resources to continuously self-renew their knowledge background and skills repository, related both to vertical and technical fields, and to transversal and communication fields. This not only enhances social inclusion, active citizenship and personal development, but also competitiveness and employability.

The potential of innovation and value generation deriving from the impact of these dynamic learning processes on the entire organizational areas and business configuration has not been fully exploited yet.

Resistance to change of people, the increasing complexity of business scenarios, and the big and profound transformations enabled by the ICT within social, business and public life, are generating a sort of "organizational myopia" that hinders the effective orchestration of the alignment between business strategy and learning strategy. In this situation, stimulating individual, organizational and inter-organizational lifelong learning proves to be a powerful lever to inject new energies and innovate products and services. This represents a big challenge for CLOs (Chief Learning Officers), CKOs (Chief Knowledge Officers), human resources managers, learning designers, and teachers, professors and experts as well.

The authors of this book propose a systemic model to activate and sustain learning processes, mainly into the higher education and adult fields.

The proposed model is also perfectly aligned with the basic principles of the Lisbon's Strategy and the lifelong learning paradigm that are promoted and supported by the European Union.

The authors call this model *"i-Learning Model"*, where *"i"* stands for:

- *"Innovation"*, to characterize the multi-faceted innovative features within an open and networked environment, and
- *"Incubator"*, to introduce the new holistic environments in which learning processes should happen.

A process-based perspective and a technology-based perspective of the i-Learning model is also provided.

The model realizes a set of integrated and synergic interventions based on six main key dimensions:

- The rethinking of curricula architecture and competence profiles, through a balanced mix of technical disciplines and soft skills (i.e., critical thinking, communication skills, mind flexibility, foreign languages fluency and international issues understanding);
- The development of a new mindset within involved people and actors, based on openness, networking, and lifelong learning;
- The innovation of learning approaches and strategies;
- The adoption of new technologies enabling new models of collaboration, knowledge creation, diffusion and access;
- The evolution of traditional learning environments based on a fixed and static concept of time and space, into stimulating, dynamic, exciting, creative, adventurous, rigorous, demanding, and empowering workplaces, active laboratories, and informal learning settings;
- The integration of the old fashioned set of metrics, mainly based on formal theoretical examinations and no-contextualized assessment, with a new set of metrics based on the capacity to design and realize valuable projects, and to build and participate actively into knowledge and learning communities, building networks and relationships. These dimensions represent the operational areas in which realizing a paradigm shift in learning.

Finally, the *"i-Learning Model"* has been also supported by an operational tool useful to design and represent an "i-Learning experience". This tool is constituted by a radar diagram with six trajectories, as shown in figure below: *interactivity, immediacy, internetworking, individualization, interdisciplinarity,* and *interoperability (*"i-Learning Radar"). It is not a case that these keywords start with the *"i"* letter: they want to contribute to clarify more the theoretical discussion of the model, and to help researchers, experts, institutions, training departments, managers and executives, professionals and instructional designers to operationalize the model, so creating innovative learning experiences and new emerging profiles. At this purpose, the book discusses also the arising of the *"Π-shaped"* professionals, a new archetype that represents an evolution of the *"T-shaped"* people, in the era of the lifelong learning.

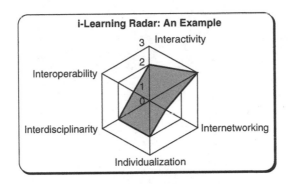

Chapter 1 is completely devoted to present the *"i-Learning Model"*in detail.

Chapters 2, 3, 4 and 5 present the instances of the model applied in different contexts (academic or corporate), involving heterogeneous targets (students, employees or young managers), in different knowledge domains. These chapters give evidence on the feasibility and applicability of the "i-Learning Model" for developing new professional profiles. As shown below, each chapter is characterized by its own i-Learning Radar.

Finally, Chap. 6 outlines future trends for designing better "i-Learning" experiences. Specifically, these trends concern technological and institutional issues. As far as the former, the adoption of promising technologies mainly related to the *Future Internet Technological Framework* is discussed. At this purpose, the concepts of *Personal Learning Environment* (PLE) and *Cloud Computing*, with some deepening on *Mobile Learning Environments* (MLE) and *3D Learning Environments* (3DLE) are particularly deepened. As concerning the institutional issues, the emerging *"Stakeholder University"* archetype is presented as the model of the University of the twenty-first century. Coherently with the lifelong learning paradigm, it could be considered as the model in which the traditional Training Departments or Corporate Universities archetypes can converge. The inspiring principles of the Stakeholder University are openness, networking, interdisciplinary and value-orientation.

Prof. Aldo Romano
President of DHITECH Scarl
(District of High Technologies)
(www.dhitech.it) - Italy

Preface

The book is structured in six chapters. Specifically, Chap. 1 presents the open networked model enabling i-learning processes. This model is further applied in four cases that are described in Chaps. 2–5. Finally, Chap. 6 discusses future trends impacting on "next-gen" learning.

The following figure gives a graphical representation of the book's architecture.

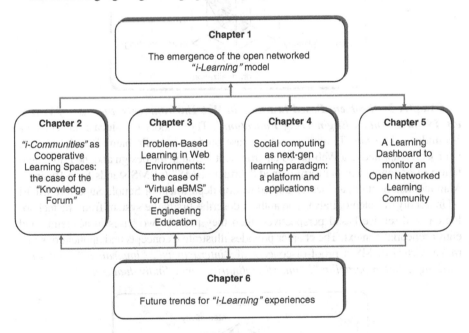

Chapter 1: *"The emergence of the Open Networked i-Learning Model"*. The author Gianluca Elia provides an overall description of the model, highlighting the process-based perspective and the technology-based perspective. The chapter introduces the model moving from the main changes happening in ICT sector, in Management, as well as in Society and Workplace. Moreover, the proposed model contributes to shape a new professional archetype for leading change, named *"Π-shaped" people*. Finally, it is also presented the *"i-Learning Radar"*, an

operational graph with six trajectories *(interdisciplinarity, interactivity, internet-working, individualization, immediacy, interoperability)* useful to design and represent an *"i-Learning experience"*.

Chapter 2: *"i-Communities as Cooperative Learning Spaces: the case of the Knowledge Forum".* The author Antonella Poce highlights mainly the concept of *interactivity*, by introducing the *"i-Communities"* as cooperative and interactive learning spaces. She presents the pedagogical foundations of the *"i-Communities"*, the new role of the involved actors, the change of strategy, the different approach to contents and to the use of technology, the updated conception of space and time characterizing the learning dynamics. Finally, a case study named *"Knowledge Forum"* is presented to highlight the main knowledge- and learning-based advantages carried out by this new kind of communities.

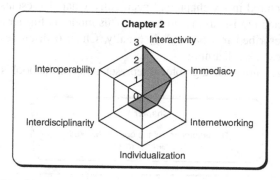

Chapter 3: *"Problem-Based Learning in Web Environments: the case of Virtual eBMS for Business Engineering Education".* The authors Gianluca Elia, Giustina Secundo and Cesare Taurino present a case study where Problem Based Learning approach is applied to a Web-based environment, through the design and the implementation of an innovative platform named "Virtual eBMS" (eBMS stands for e-Business Management Section, a research and education department of Scuola Superiore ISUFI – University of Salento, Italy). The authors describe firstly the system from the technological and service based perspectives; then they present two cases in academic and entrepreneurial context. The chapter provides illustrative concepts and applications that make Virtual eBMS a proof-of-concept of *"interactivity"*, *"immediacy"*, *"internet-working"*, *"interoperability"*, *"interdisciplinarity"*, and *"individualization"*.

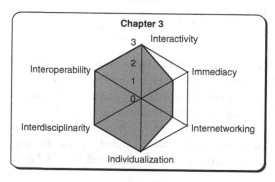

Chapter 4: *"Social computing as next-gen learning paradigm: a platform and applications"*. The authors Alessandro Margherita, Cesare Taurino and Pasquale Del Vecchio discuss how individuals and groups interact for learning and working purposes, through the generation of Internet applications tagged as web 2.0. In this chapter, the authors describe an innovative platform (named "WeLearn") designed and implemented to support a case-based and project-driven learning strategy. A set of illustrative scenarios are described, for the development of business and technology management competencies in undergraduate and graduate education programs. This chapter highlights five dimensions of the implemented i-learning model presented in the first chapter: *"interactivity"*, *"immediacy"*, *"inter-networking"*, *"interoperability"* and *"individualization"*.

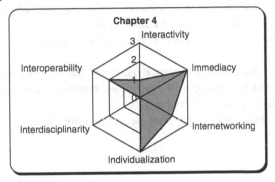

Chapter 5: *"A Learning Dashboard to monitor an Open Networked Learning Community"*. The authors Francesca Grippa, Giustina Secundo and Marco De Maggio propose an operational model to monitor and assess an Open Networked i-Learning Community. Specifically, the model is based on the Intellectual Capital framework, and it relies on the social network analysis to map several and complementary perspectives of a learning network. The chapter highlights three fundamental dimensions of the open networked i-learning model: *"internetworking"*, *"interactivity"* and *"individualization"*.

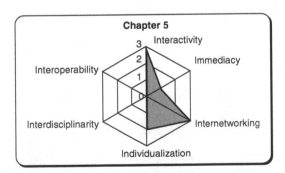

Chapter 6: *"Future Trends for i-Learning Experiences"*. The authors Gianluca Elia and Antonella Poce outline future technological and organizational trends for designing better *"i-Learning"* experiences. Technological trends are mainly related

to the Future Internet technological framework, and they underline the concepts of *Personal Learning Environment* (PLE) and *Cloud Computing*, with some deepening on *Mobile Learning Environments* (MLE) and *3D Learning Environments* (3DLE). Organizational trends are focused on presenting the emerging of the *"Stakeholder University"* archetype as emerging model to support competence development processes in twenty-first century.

Feedback

We are interested in hearing your comments about this book and about the effectiveness of your applications of the "i-Learning Model".

Your suggestions and your work will contribute significantly in realizing a society.

Our hope is to share with the reader feedback and insights that contribute to shape a world in which learning is like the air we breathe, and effective application of knowledge is like our heart that beat.

This will make better our society, our people and our planet.

Acknowledgements

This book is the result of a collective work, made implicitly and explicitly by all the authors and their respective research groups.

Without their passion, their exciting work, their continuous provocations and insights, this book would not exist.

A special thanks to Prof. Aldo Romano, a visionary and open-minded entrepreneur in learning field, convinced supporter of creative destruction processes inspired to a Schumpeterian view of innovation, and real inspirer and hidden director of this work. His suggestions and his way of thinking "out-of-schema" have been the main sources of energy to write this book.

We would thank also Prof. Giuseppina Passiante and Prof. Ernesto Damiani, for their precious suggestions, scientific recommendations and continuous support they provided for this work.

A remarkable appreciation to Prof. Benedetto Vertecchi and Prof. Gilly Salmon for their researches and studies that have inspired the pedagogical soul of this book.

A great recognition to the technicians of the Euro-Mediterranean Incubator of Scuola Superiore ISUFI (University of Salento), especially the "hardware, networking & security" team, the "software architecture & development" group, and the "web learning" staff: their professionalism, patience and spirit of sacrifice are at the basis of the successes we reached together.

This book represents also a result of the project *"eLD@Med.Net – eLearning for Development"*, a research project funded by the Italian Ministry for Education and Research aimed at developing an integrated system of e-Learning and Knowledge Management supporting innovation in the learning processes into the Mediterranean space.

A remarkable thanks to the learners, technicians, researchers, professors vice-presidents, presidents and directors of Universities, Institutions and Technoparks of the Southern Mediterranean Countries with which many of the authors had (and continue to have) the pleasure to collaborate: Al Akhawayn University (Morocco), The University of Jordan (Jordan), Jordan Education Initiative (JEI), Technopole Elgazala (Tunisia), Casablanca Technopark (Morocco), Arab Academy for e-Business (Syria), CGEM (Morocco), ANPME (Morocco), CTICI (Tunisia), IHEC Cartage (Tunisia), and many others organizations that represent a first nucleus of partners on the road of the "i-learning" experiences. With them, we continue to work for designing jointly the future of our collaboration.

Contents

Contents

List of Contributors

Pasquale Del Vecchio holds a Ph.D. from the Euro-Mediterranean Incubator of Scuola Superiore ISUFI – University of Salento (Italy) where he is currently a Researcher. In 2007, he was a visiting Ph.D. student at the MIT Sloan Center for Digital Business. His research is focused on Social Network Analysis applications to virtual communities enabled by the use of Web 2.0 tools, mainly in marketing. Currently, he's involved in research activities focused on interdisciplinary and competence-based learning approaches to Business Management (pasquale.delvecchio@ebms.unile.it).

Marco De Maggio holds a Ph.D. from the Euro-Mediterranean Incubator of Scuola Superiore ISUFI – University of Salento (Italy) where he is currently a Researcher. In 2007, he was a visiting Ph.D. student at the MIT Sloan Center for Digital Business. His research concerns the development of methodologies for the analysis and management of learning patterns within organizations and communities of practice. Currently, he's involved in the development of an interdisciplinary approach and competence development models in higher and management education (marco.demaggio@ebms.unile.it).

Gianluca Elia is Assistant Professor at the Faculty of Engineering and at the Department of Innovation Engineering of University of Salento (Italy), where he teaches *"Internet Business Models and Tools"* and other topics related to *"Business Engineering"* field. He is also strongly involved in the research activities related to *"Learning Systems Engineering"* at the Euro Mediterranean Incubator – University of Salento (www.ebms.it), where he also coordinates the *"Mediterranean School of e-Business Management"* initiative. His research interests concern the innovative methodologies, strategies and tools enabling collaborative learning processes. He has been also involved in the design and management of complex research projects focused on the integration of Web Learning, Knowledge Management and e-Business fields, in collaboration with leading companies, universities and research centers. He had also a major role in the design and implementation of the "Virtual eBMS", a technological platform integrating knowledge management and web learning applications. This platform was awarded the "Brandon Hall Research" prize in learning technology in 2006 (gianluca.elia@unisalento.it).

Francesca Grippa holds a Ph.D. and a MSc from the Euro-Mediterranean Incubator of Scuola Superiore ISUFI – University of Salento (Italy) where she is currently a Researcher. In 2005 and 2006, she was a visiting Ph.d. student at the MIT Sloan Center for Digital Business. Her research interests include the application of Social Network Analysis to business and learning communities (francesca.grippa@ebms.unile.it).

Alessandro Margherita holds a Ph.D. and a MSc from the Euro-Mediterranean Incubator of Scuola Superiore ISUFI – University of Salento (Italy) where currently he is a Researcher. His research activities have a cross-disciplinary business and technology management focus. He has an interest in the fields of organizational change based on technology adoption and process redesign, and organizational development through learning and competency growth. He's involved in the design and experimentation of innovative methodologies, models and technology platforms to support higher education and corporate learning processes. He also collaborates with the MIT Sloan Center for Digital Business, where he was visiting Ph.D. student in 2006 (alessandro.margherita@ebms.unile.it).

Antonella Poce is a full time researcher in experimental pedagogy at the University Roma Tre – Department for Educational Design. After concluding the PhD in Innovation and evaluation of educational system, she obtained a post-doc scholarship for carrying out research on the evaluation of e-learning models in university didactics. Her research interests concern the evaluation of innovative didactic practices in university education at national and European level. On the same topic, she has participated in several national and international research projects. She was awarded by Aea-Europe for her research activities. She is a member of the Aea_Europe subcommittee for Professional Development (poce@uniroma3.it).

Giustina Secundo holds a MSc from the Euro-Mediterranean Incubator of Scuola Superiore ISUFI – University of Salento (Italy), where currently she is Assistant Professor in Business Engineering. Her research interest concerns the emerging trends in management education and human capital creation process in business schools and corporations, with a special focus on the evolution of corporate university phenomenon. These research activities are strictly connected to her involvement in the management of the advanced education programs of the Incubator, involving students coming from Tunisia, Morocco and Jordan. She's a lecturer of Innovation Management and Project Management at the Faculty of Engineering of the University of Salento since 2001 (giusy.secundo@ebms.unile.it).

Cesare Taurino after a Degree in Computer Science Engineering, started his professional experience as a Research Fellow at the Euro-Mediterranean Incubator of Scuola Superiore ISUFI – University of Salento (Italy). His research is focused on

emerging trends, methodologies and technologies for web learning, including the implication of semantic web paradigm. As a responsible of the Web Learning Lab of the eBMS, he's involved in the management, customization and administration of the eBMS Web Learning platform, as well as in the creation of learning contents delivered through the platform
(cesare.taurino@ebms.unile.it).

Chapter 1
The Emergence of the Open Networked "i-Learning" Model

Gianluca Elia

Abstract The most significant forces that are changing the business world and the society behaviors in this beginning of the twenty-first century can be identified into the globalization of the economy, technological evolution and convergence, change of the workers' expectations, workplace diversity and mobility, and mostly, knowledge and learning as major organizational assets. But which type of learning dynamics must be nurtured and pursued within the organizations, today, in order to generate valuable knowledge and its effective applications? After a brief discussion on the main changes observable in management, ICT and society/workplace in the last years, this chapter aims to answer to this question, through the proposition of the "Π-shaped" profile (a new professional archetype for leading change), and through the discussion of the open networked "i-Learning" model (a new framework to "incubate" innovation in learning processes). Actually, the "i" stands for "innovation" (to highlight the nature of the impact on traditional learning model), but also it stands for "incubation" (to underline the urgency to have new environments in which incubating new professional profiles). Specifically, the main key characteristics at the basis of the innovation of the learning processes will be presented and described, by highlighting the managerial, technological and societal aspects of their nature. A set of operational guidelines will be also provided to activate and sustain the innovation process, so implementing changes in the strategic dimensions of the model. Finally, the "i-Learning Radar" is presented as an operational tool to design, communicate and control an "i-Learning experience". This tool is represented by a radar diagram with six strategic dimensions of a learning initiative.

Keywords i-Learning • Radical innovation in human capital creation • T-shaped people • Π-shaped people • Learning incubator • Learner-centered communities • Personal learning environment • Personal learning network

G. Elia (✉)
Euro-Mediterranean Incubator – Department of Engineering Innovation,
University of Salento, Lecce, Italy
e-mail: gianluca.elia@unisalento.it

G. Elia and A. Poce (eds.), *Open Networked "i-Learning": Models and Cases of "Next-Gen" Learning*, DOI 10.1007/978-1-4419-6854-8_1,
© Springer Science+Business Media, LLC 2010

1 The Main On-Going Changes in ICT, Management and Society/Workplace

Today, competitive scenario is characterised by an increasing complexity and a set of revolutionary processes (Marquardt 2002), like:

- A rapid transition from an industrial society into a knowledge society in which knowledge represents the fourth production factor (and the most important one), and learning is the most strategic process.
- The increasing technological development and convergence causing the transformation of the "spatial and time proximities" into a "relational proximity", with a great impact on the people's workplace and mobility.
- The disappearing of borders among organizations, industries and countries that generates a global competition with growing opportunities and threats.
- The evolution of the organizations towards open environments characterized by global vision, involvement of heterogeneous actors, technology as a pervasive facility, collaboration, knowledge sharing, internal/external social network exploitation.

The mutual influence of these forces and the generated effects have been interpreted by Dunning as the emergence of a new form of capitalism called "Flexible Capitalism" (Dunning 1997), and that substitutes the old existing forms of capitalism characterizing the competitive dynamics until early 1980. For Dunning, the radical changes underpinning the new capitalism are related to the evolution processes influencing multiple businesses and economical dimensions, as it is shown in Table 1.1.

These changes generate dynamic and hyper competitive markets, local and global at the same time, strongly based on the exploitation and exploration of intangible assets, on knowledge exchanges and applications, and on value creation

Table 1.1 Phases of evolution in modern capitalism

Dimension	Entrepreneurial capitalism	Hierarchical capitalism	Flexible capitalism
Period	(1770–1875)	(1875–1980)	(1980–?)
Markets	Small, fragmented, local	National/ international	Global and integrated
Cooperation and competition	Single entrepreneurs, small companies	Oligopoly	Dynamism and hyper-competition
Organization	Small organizations	Hierarchies	Strategic alliances
Key resource	Natural resources	Physical capital	Tangible/intangible assets
Asset mobility	Low	Medium	High for firm-specific assets
Government role	Limited involvement	Welfare state	Participation and support
Cross-national integration	Financial markets	Discontinuous	High interconnection
Hegemonic power	UK	USA	None

processes, where the concept of value is related not only to the economical and financial issues, but also to social perspective.

In these markets, the ICT – and the Internet in particular – represent the endogenous factor triggering to a socio-economic and cultural "revolution" that has just began. Actually, according to the structuralist-evolutionary theory (Freeman and Perez 1988; Lipsey 1998) the ICT behave as an enabling technology that affects the whole economy and drastically alters societies through their impact on pre-existing economic and social structures. In the past, according to this vision, examples of other enabling technologies have been "material technologies", "energy technologies", and "transportation technologies".

Aligned to this interpretation, ICT and the Internet can be considered as a *"General Purpose Technology"* that affects business dynamics, social behaviors, communication patterns, cultural models, innovation practices, value creation processes (McKnight et al. 2001).

This interpretation brings to the consideration that today ICT and the Internet are totally embedded in all the aspects of the social and business life. Actually, it's impossible to conceptualize and design any business initiatives and strategies that have not embedded a pervasive ICT infrastructure and an Internet-based architecture as their main background (Tapscott 2006). So, today ICT and the Internet can be conceived as fundamental enablers of social and business interactions, as well as the role of materials, energies and electricity, and transportation for the companies of 1960s–1970s–1980s.

More in particular, the revolutionary effect of the Internet and its impact on management issues and social aspects, is mainly due to its main key features (Afuah and Tucci 2003):

- *Networking and Mediating Technology.* Internet connects people and organizations, independently on their physical location or time reference. It creates new interfaces enabling global collaboration and relationships. It develops new business opportunities among private and public stakeholders, and citizens (Business-to-Business; Business-to-Consumer; Consumer-to-Consumer; Business to Employees, Business-to-Government; Government-to-Government).
- *Infinite Virtual Capacity.* The Internet infrastructure allows for storing a huge amount of digitized "products" and "services". Digital warehouses constitute a big opportunity to attract the interest of every kind of customers, so creating an infinite catalogue of potential businesses. In this way, virtual environments arise, in which choice and abundance coexist, leaving the central role to the customer's attention.
- *Low Cost Standard.* Accessing to the Internet is today a "commodity", a basic condition to access to a bundle of value added services. The revolutionary discovery of the TCP/IP protocol made in early 1970s by DARPA (Defence Advanced Research Project Agency) opened immense spaces for communicating and collaborating, for offering new products and services, or for innovating existing way to offer traditional products and services. Participating to the Web is not an expensive condition: it is necessary a minimum investment of money and a huge investment in creativity and entrepreneurship.

- *Information Asymmetry Shrinker.* Internet makes public many "secrets" that in the past guaranteed sustainability to no-adding value operators. Thanks to the Internet, everyone is capable to gather autonomously information and taking decisions. This process transfers the bargaining power to the customers, who can conduit and make their choices considering the real value of each single transaction. Scarcity of information resources doesn't belong to the Internet era, where the law of increasing returns regulates the entire business. The "attention" is the real scarce resource and on which organizations are focusing by offering to customers not more a product or a service, but a very unique and personalized experience, relevant, appropriate, convenient and attractive.
- *Creative Destroyer.* Internet opens new opportunities and chances that were unimaginable and unthinkable before. According to the neo-Schumpeterian view (Dosi et al. 1988), as a large technological innovation, Internet is "destroying" entire industries (such as music), it is radically modifying other ones (such as travel agencies or publishing), and it is opening new ones (such as on line advertising or virtual malls). Internet allows a network-based organization that exploits virtualness as main principle for coordination and business execution. Extremely thinking, a "one-person organization" is capable to carry on business at global scale, through pursuing outsourcing strategies and strengthening strategic partnerships and alliances.
- *Transaction Cost Reducer/Disintermediation.* Internet enables easily disintermediation amongst producers and consumers, cutting down sensibly the number of no-adding value intermediaries, leveraging on efficient logistics. Besides, it reduces drastically transaction costs facilitating and accelerating searching, contracting and coordinating activities (Coase 1937).
- *Network Externalities.* Internet favours the diffusion of information at wide scale, so directly or indirectly promoting products and services. This process accelerates the large scale adoption and usage of products, so augmenting their potential and intrinsic value.

After the discovery of the transistor and the birth of the integrated circuits (end of 1950s), the invention of the microprocessor (early 1970s) and the diffusion of PC (1980s), probably the next "discontinuity" in the evolution process of the ICT is represented by the wide access to Internet from the major part of the population (mid 1990s).

Along the time, this diffusion activated two parallel processes:

- From one side, the systematic *technological convergence* amongst contents industry, telecommunication industry and computers.
- From the other side, the diffusion of the *"network" paradigm* as new flexible organizational model enabling collaboration and communication, in which digitized information and real time processing play a fundamental role for coordination.

These two technology-enabled processes generated a mindset shift in daily life, in social behaviors, in customer habits. Irremediably this influenced also radically the management styles and approaches.

By summarizing in one single concept, referring to the studies of Dosi and his colleagues in eighties, it is possible to interpret the digital revolution of the twenty-first century as a new *"techno-economic paradigm"* that creates new markets, new products and services, new organizational forms, new management styles, new professional profiles (Dosi et al. 1988). The central technology of this phenomenon is no longer the one related to the automation of the production processes, but it is the one linked to communication and information processing.

1.1   Changes in ICT

By following a phenomenological approach to present and introduce the revolutionary changes happened (and happening) in ICT industry, it could be interesting to reflect on three "evidence-based" laws related to progresses in Computing Power, in Network Value, and in Connection Speed. Respectively the three laws are the *Moore's law*, the *Metcalfe's law* and the *Gilder's law*.

Moore's Law (1965) is the law that impacts on the *Computing Power*. According to the original form of this law, the number of transistors per square inch on integrated circuits had doubled every 18 months, so the processing power of a microchip doubles every 18 months. Starting from this original formulation, the corollary states that at constant price, computers double in speed every 18 months and the price of a given level of computing power halves every 18 months. This generates great implications in terms of computing power and processing capabilities.

Metcalfe's Law (1980) is the law that impacts on the *Network Value*. According to the original form of this law, the value of a telecommunications network is proportional to the square of the number of connected users of the system. After the explosion of the Internet and WWW (World Wide Web), the focus of the law shifted from the value of the telecommunications network to the value of organizational network and community. So, today, the corollary states that the community value of a network grows as the square of the number of its users increase, while the cost per user remains the same or even reduces.

Gilder's Law (2000) is the law that impacts on the *Connection Speed*. According to this law, the bandwidth of communication systems grows at least three times faster than computer power. This means that if computer power doubles every 18 months (Moore's Law), the bandwidth of communications systems doubles every 6 months.

These three laws highlight a deep and fast technological (r)evolution respectively in computing power, network-based value and connection speed, with a parallel decrease of costs to participate actively in the Internet era.

These three laws are on the basis of the other phenomenon that characterize today's Internet era. Let's think of the growth of mobile technologies and devices, and their rapid adoption from the entire society. Let's think to the explosion of digital contents industry, or to the diffusion of Internet, Extranet and Intranet configuration amongst business actors and communities. Let's consider the pervasive adoption of ICT-based application to manage a company or an institution at intra- and inter-organizational level (ERP systems, CRM tools, integrated e-Business platforms, Business Intelligence suites, etc.). Let's think to the development of methodologies, techniques and tools enabling Document Management systems, Knowledge Management suites, Workflow Management tools, Collaborative Working Environments, Web Learning platforms.

Alongside these "continuous" and "pervasive" realities and examples, there is a mine of numerous products, services, or processes that embed the ICT revolutions and that form part of everyday life. One for all is Google that, based on high-performing technological infrastructure (hardware, software and network) valorizes the power of users' behaviors and communities' contributions to increase the quality of the services offered and to create new business opportunities.

PlayStation 3 represents a product enabled by the high-performing computing power of processors. File-sharing communities and peer-to-peer services exploit the value of the network, not only in terms of speed but mainly in terms of number of participating users. The same for on line communities like e-Bay or e-Lance that generates value (for itself and for its members) mainly based on the active participation of a huge number of "instantaneous" and highly loyal customers and suppliers.

What is written above represents only a "screenshot" of a today's scene. If we assist to the entire movie, we can perceive future trends in ICT (r)evolution and their strong convergence and integration with the *nano-bio-cogno technologies*.

This trend confirms the profound transformation that ICT are living: their acronym stands for *Information and Communication Technologies*, but it is transforming into *Integration and Collaboration Technologies*.

This shift is an expression of a reality we are assisting to. Actually, through the ICT it is possible not only to transfer information and to enable communication amongst people and/or machines; this is just a commodity. ICT can process information, enable knowledge application, manage competencies, skills and experiences, organize people and projects, solve problems. Today ICT enhance interactivity in communication, they enable heterogeneous systems to collaborate each other in a single integrated architecture, by configuring and offering to knowledge workers customized desktop-workspaces combining different and heterogeneous services, accessible every time and everywhere. Three-dimensional environments and immersive simulations offer new opportunities to make more effective every ICT-enabled experience. On line applications and remote services share the same virtual space and interact each other – and with knowledge workers – to solve problems and delivery solutions.

This "integrated" vision is further supported by the integrated access to channels and devices; knowledge workers can easily use traditional wired or wireless internet connections, but also through mobile networks, digital TV, or satellite links. Devices can be traditional personal computers (workstation or notebook), but also mobile phones, personal digital assistants (PDAs), tablet PC, smart phones, interactive TV, Wii and other game consoles. This perspective of ICT usage confirms their characteristics and role of "Integration" and "Collaboration" facilitating structure.

1.2 Changes in Management

Normally, the term *"Management"* is commonly used to explicit the capability of people to organize tangible and intangible resources for reaching a specific goal and objectives. Embedded in the term, there is a set of implicit behaviors and activities that characterize the role of manager, such as planning, organizing, staffing, coordinating. directing, monitoring, controlling, motivating, coaching, etc.

So, the term "management" assumes implicitly the presence of something or a context that already exists, to be analyzed before to be managed. So, a manager analyzes the context, he balances opportunities and threats, he evaluates strengths and weaknesses, and finally he decides and executes. Normally, manager operates according to a "reactive" strategy, assuming that the world is linear, static and highly rational (Romano et al. 2009).

This view of management is basically due to the managers' primary goals to allocate scarce resources, to assign punctual responsibilities, and to monitor performance through sophisticated control systems. This approach to management is coherent with the System–Strategy–Structure (3S) model (Ghoshal and Bartlett 1999). The model reveals its effectiveness in static contexts, where fixed and planned strategies are put in practice. The 3S model is gradually evolving towards People–Purpose–Process (3P) model, typical of every changing contexts. This model highlights two fundamental concepts: (a) the locus of knowledge production and innovation is the human resource, and (b) the role of organization is to stimulate people's creativity and to create environments enabling new initiatives, cooperation and learning. This evolution sees, respectively, "Structure" dimension that shifts to "Process" dimension, highlighting the transformation of hierarchical configuration and fixed coordination mechanism to a more fluid organization where the process perspective is aligned to responsibility and value generation function.

"Strategy" shifts to "Purpose", to underline the evolution of the role of managers: from designers of corporate strategies to shapers of institutional purposes; the traditional sense of opportunities that inspires the design of corporate strategies evolves towards the sense of responsibility that highlights the moral contract of managers with the organization.

Finally, "System" evolves to "People" to make more effective, valuable and faster the decision making processes. This shift presupposes the empowerment of people as main decision makers of daily operations, so facing fast changing environmental demands and opportunities.

Figure 1.1 highlights the 3S–3P paradigm shift in management (Ghoshal and Bartlett 1999).

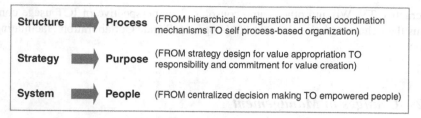

Fig. 1.1 The 3S–3P paradigm shift in management

In performing their new roles, managers have to change their priorities and become themselves builders of the organization. They have also to address their efforts in creating a sense of meaning within the company that members can clearly identify and in which they will feel free to share ideas and commitment (Ghoshal and Bartlett 1999).

In the 3S–3P shift, Ghoshal and Bartlett identify the profile of the *"Individualized Corporation"*, by arguing that the results that managers will reach are a consequence of their capability of attracting, motivating, developing, and retaining individuals. Their style can be assimilated to the one presented by Thomas Malone in his book *"The Future of Work – How the New Order of Business Will Shape Your Organization, Your Management Style, and Your Life"* (Malone 2004), where he highlights the major value created through *coordinating-and-cultivating* strategy rather than *command-and-control* approach. He presents the new role of manager not as a new one, but as an evolution of the previous one: this means that coordinating and cultivating are not the opposite of commanding and controlling. Rather, they are supersets that encompass commanding and controlling, as well as many other management approaches. On the other dimension there is the degree of centralization. So it's fundamental to find a right balance between centralized and decentralized mechanisms to implement coordination. This depends mainly on the activities to be done, on the relationships among them, on the flows of information exchanged, and on the people who do the activities. Effective implementation of the coordinating-and-cultivating approach is the result of an intelligent mix among capabilities, incentives and connections (for coordinating activities), and of harnessing of natural tendencies, blooming of thousand flowers, encouraging cross-fertilization and information exchanges (for nurturing people).

But the digital revolution, interpreted as a new techno-economic paradigm, enabled (a) new organizational forms based on network configuration and (b) global competitive scenarios in which knowledge represents the most critical and valuable (not scarce) resource, and learning the core process. These two effects caused a general increase of complexity, chaos and uncertainty mainly in those businesses characterized by high-speed interactions, openness, peering sharing and global action (Tapscott and Williams 2006).

Thus, the new approach to management should face the challenges of the emerging digital economy (Tapscott 1996). Actually, the traditional concept of *time* is completely revolutionized (real-time transaction enabled by the ICT; high frequency of changes; shortening of life-cycles of products, services, markets and competencies). *Space* has become a relative concept; "virtualness" overcomes geogr aphical positions, and promotes organizational and relational proximity. The increased interconnections inside and among organizations confirm the network as a value-oriented organizational form, and the *density* as a key variable to measure the openness of the structures. *Diversity* due to the proliferation of heterogeneous and self-organizing agents with highly specific and independent behavior causes the emergence of a complex economic and business scenario whose state in many cases is close to the chaos.

Coherently, new management approaches and styles need to evolve according to these new complex scenarios. From one side a manager has to master the engagements, the decisions and the actions designed and executed to gain competitive advantage; from the other side he has to identify new business opportunities and to pursue them through new configurations of tangible and intangible resources. These two perspectives merge two complementary fields: the Strategic Management and the Entrepreneurship (Hitt et al. 2001, 2002; Venkatraman and Sarasvathy 2001).

Coherently with the digital and knowledge economy scenario, we should interpret a manager as an *"entrepreneurial manager"*, capable to:

– Anticipate and adapt readily the strategy to environmental and industry changes.
– Accelerate the development of new products, processes and services.
– Expedite the transfer of individual and organizational knowledge.
– Learn more effectively from the past and from the environment.
– Shorten the time needed to implement strategic changes.
– Stimulate continuous improvement organization-wide.
– Promote distributed leadership.
– Attract best human resource and constantly develop people at all levels.
– Stimulate commitment and creativity.
– Define simple strategies with limited number of guidelines.
– Pursue a logic of stakeholder value creation as the real foundation of success.

Definitively, the entrepreneurial manager should define a dynamic and adaptable strategy, adopting a proactive behavior to identify potential opportunities of value creation, focusing on fast and distributed decision making process, strengthening alliances and partnerships with key stakeholders, balancing risk through the definition of few simple rules and the set up of few core processes. Preferably, he should be able to impose the pace of change and to renew the rules of the game.

The entrepreneurial manager, thus, should promote the *4S organizational model*: *Single-minded* about its core business, *Speedy* in its response to all stimuli, *Sociable* in its maintenance of friendly relations, partnerships and alliances inside and outside the firm, and *Shallow* in its structure. An organization that becomes a "living being", in which the real value is embedded in its people who promote radical paradigm shifts: command-and-control approach evolves towards coordination-and-nurturing, self-organization and commitment; hierarchical structure towards spider organizations and collaborative networks; make-and-sell approach toward sense-and-seize strategy; performance based on profitability toward value based on innovation and growth.

In implementing these paradigm shifts within complex, multi-stakeholders and high-speed scenarios, the mindset and the mental models of the entrepreneurial managers have to make a quantum leap. They have to balance and mix rightly a Newtonian approach based on linear thinking, determinism, predictable goals, quantifiable and controllable features with a non-linear and ever-changing approach characterized by flexibility, adaptive behaviors and dynamic capabilities (Teece et al. 1997).

They have to "navigate" in chaotic and changing environments characterized by wide opened and highly interconnected systems; adoption of simple rules and dynamic capabilities to manage this complexity reveals the only way to replace forecasting strategies with foresight strategies (Eisenhardt and Sull 2001).

1.3   Changes in Society and Workplace

The third typology of changes analyzed in this chapter concerns the social perspective and its impact on the workplace, but not because it is the less important; on the contrary, social changes can be seen as a "measure" of the impact of the ICT and management changes. At the same time, they also influence them strongly, since they reveal normal and/or emerging behaviors of customers, citizens, companies and institutions.

Nowadays, ICT-based services, Internet based tools and (mobile) technological devices are commonly used by a large number of users to perform daily their working tasks and personal engagements. This great and rapid diffusion has been facilitated by the reduction of the buying costs of the equipment, and mainly by the decreasing of the costs to access to the web and to related services.

Always-on access to e-mail, instant messenger, phone lines, search engines, yellow and blue pages, personal agenda … on line communities, social networking spaces … knowledge repositories, learning bases … interactive games … multimedia contents … create a sense of "urgency", a sort of "unbridled need" to access immediately to contents, people and services, a kind of "anxiety" to receive immediately a feedback from other people and technological systems.

This phenomenon is further characterized by the fact that users adopt several typologies of devices to access to the services and contents (portable devices like mobile phone, PDA, smart phone, notebook, PC … interactive TV, play-station … but also mini-computer on board to cars and boats, or computerized health systems pluggable to gym machines, restaurant tables …). Often, these devices can be synchronized among them, so generating a sort of global "intelligent", "networked" and "virtual" environment in which people are immersed and where they work, interact, communicate, enjoy, plan, organize … live.. embedding ICT and Internet.

In this environment the traditional concepts of time and space are completely revolutionized; "workplace" is a general concept today and it is not associated to one single physical place or to a fixed time slot. New concepts are emerging: "space of flows", "space of relationships", in which the physical geographical position and the time dimension become not so much relevant compared to the value of exchanged and shared contents, knowledge, competencies and skills, experiences, opportunities, and ideas.

"Flexibility" is another characteristic of this environment. It is not important "where" people perform their tasks, but it is strategic "how" they do their job, the level of satisfaction of their (internal/external) customers, and mainly the competencies developed during the task, potentially replicable to perform similar future jobs.

Openness, *peering* and *sharing* (Tapscott and Williams 2006) are three fundamental values and principles that drive people in this environment. They really contribute to create trust among individuals, to valorise diversity and density, favouring interactive, effective and immediate (on demand) communication.

Single expertise is continuously replaced by *collective intelligence* that emerges from mass collaboration and virtuous competition of many individuals.

It is the time that Tapscott defines as *"Age of Networked Intelligence"* (Tapscott 1996), an era characterized by the generation of a new economy, a new politic, a new society, new behaviors, new values, new cultures, etc. An era strongly characterized by the "abundance", and in which the main scarce resource is the "attention". Actually, the choice becomes the instant in which customer configures and personalizes his products and services, through a collaborative process of design (and often also implementation) that eliminates the distance between producer and consumer.

Customization phase is the moment in which customer realizes a balance between individual preferences and community trends. Today, personalization is the "killer" application to succeed, since it allows to conjugate the identity of the subject with the sense of belonging to the community. In the first instance, these two concepts can appear in antithesis, but their complementarity constitutes the key point of view to interpret the emerging social changes that have been significantly contributing to implement the shift from a mass market to a mass of markets, so highlighting the nowadays well known dynamics of the "long tails" phenomenon (Anderson 2006).

2   A New Professional Archetype for Leading Change

Managing the above discussed changes happening in ICT, Management and Social fields, and their impact on workplace dynamics, is a very challenging goal. Leading these changes is almost impossible!

Actually, this is a reality if we continue to think, plan and act with traditional mental schemas. Otherwise, if we adopt a new perspective and if we train our mindset within dynamic and stimulating contexts, then we will develop new knowledge, skills and attitudes that will support us in facing and leading changes successfully.

In fact, the biggest risk we can encounter is to not considering the phenomenon of competency obsolescence. Actually, similarly to products that are characterized by a specific life cycle, also knowledge and competencies have their own life cycle and so they can become "obsolete". And, since we live in a knowledge-based economy, these life cycles are narrowing more and more, so generating a sense of "urgency" in fulfilling the knowledge gap, at every level and independently on the typology of work, the geographical position, and economic or social sector. This means that today's competencies and know how are not sufficient to face tomorrow's jobs and challenges; people have to continuously update their professional profile if they want to be strategic for their organizations, and to remain competitive in the market labour.

So, learning becomes the most critical process for understanding and adapting to the ever-changing speed of change (Marquardt 2002); from a one-time based and fixed-spaced event, learning becomes a *lifelong challenge* and a *lifelong process*.

2.1 "Π-Shaped" People as Change Agent

The "output" of traditional education process is represented by people that are skilled in very few specific technical disciplines, but very weak in soft skills like communication, critical thinking, team building, leadership, etc. This trend is also confirmed by the report published by the Economist Intelligence Unit in 2008, entitled *"The Future of Higher Education"*. So, people or knowledge workers, with a professional profile characterized by a single expertise, technical skills and vertical specialization are not destined to manage and lead changes; they go and run towards the isolation, where they are unable to create value.

Otherwise, people and knowledge workers that operate as experts and generalists at the same time, skilled in a single domain but capable to interact, understand and communicate with other specialists coming from a wide range of disciplines, they have the potential to be effective change managers and leaders. This new professional archetype name *"T-shaped"* is replacing the traditional one named *"I-shaped"*. The choice of the "T" highlights the importance to have both the vertical expertise and the horizontal skills; so "T-shaped" concept embeds "I-shaped" one (Secundo et al. 2009a).

Definitively, T-shaped people operate as *"specialists"* (capable to apply specific concepts related to a well defined knowledge domain), as *"integrators"* (capable to synthesize and to merge business, social, ethical and technological issues for obtaining a team-based complex result), and as *"leaders"* (capable to manage changes, to control tension, to be creative and entrepreneurial, to perceive new insights underpinning the change, to promote proactive behaviours, to pursue value creation initiatives, to anticipate future trends, to forecast external re/actions and to foresight future scenarios).

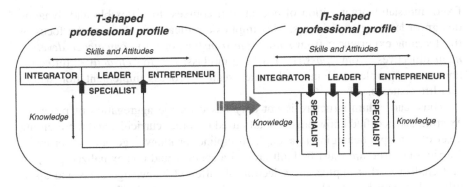

Fig. 1.2 T-shaped and Π-shaped professional profile

In T-shaped profile, the horizontal level of skills and attitudes is not what individuals develop during the work, but it represents a sort of "meta-skill" that is taught and learnt during the learning experiences. Actually, in the T-shaped profile, skills and attitudes layer is developed after the consolidation of the single vertical specialization.

More appropriately, with the increasing complexity of socio-economical scenarios, the high number of emergent disciplines and knowledge domains, the huge number of required competencies and skills necessary to perform a job, the blurring of boundaries among different sectors, a more complex profile is emerging. It represents a sort of evolution of T-shaped version towards a multi-skilled profile, where the areas of expertise increase as number, becoming less deepen (Hayashi and Kurokawa 2009), so generating multiple vertical layers. On the contrary, the horizontal layer of "skills and attitudes" is more robust and it enables individuals to self develop their competencies and reach new specializations. This new profile has been named "Π-shaped" people, a term coined in 2006 by Stuart Feldman, Vice President of Computer Science at IBM Research. "Π-shaped" professionals combine different industry-specific competencies and knowledge domains, integrating them with a balanced mix of social skills, problem solving attitudes, project oriented mindset, management style, and entrepreneurial framework, that represent the basis on which developing new further vertical specializations, according to specific needs and requests.

Figure 1.2 shows a graphical representation of the "T-shaped" and "Π-shaped" professional profile.

Creating "Π-shaped" professional implies a radical transformation of the curriculum architecture in terms of its design and delivery.

2.2 Curriculum Design and Delivery for "Π-Shaped" People

Creating new professional profile implies designing new curriculum architecture and new delivery strategies. Actually, it's fundamental to realize the shift from a fixed and static organization of educational courses, to a flexible and dynamic design of learning experiences. This implies a radical rethinking of the focus of the learning experience: from *knowledge transfer* goals to *competence development* objectives; from *"passive"* teaching in classroom to *"eff-active"* (effective and active) problem solving and value creation process implementation within real life contexts.

Thus, curriculum structure is not only based on the aggregation of pieces of existing and codified knowledge, already used for other curricula, and representing a set of concepts belonging to a single discipline, or knowledge domain, or topic. Curriculum structure must be built around a specific and contextualized problem and challenge; this implies the selection of different knowledge areas and disciplines that contribute to elaborate possible alternatives and the final solution.

Figure 1.3 gives an overview about the new curricula structure.

Moreover, this framework allows the extending of the traditional close-structured curriculum, overcoming the boundaries existing among different disciplines. Finally, it realizes also the integration of external sources of knowledge and experiences, so generating open curriculum structures that combine virtuously several distinct and complementary expertises coming from the academic institutions, the research centers, companies and industrial actors, public authorities. These categories of actors interact with learners and, jointly, they express and interpret the learning needs, they design and guide the learning paths, as well as they support and promote the learning results. Knowledge flows, active collaboration and fruitful cooperation animate the learning processes and stimulate/motivate learners in collaborating and cooperating among them and with the stakeholders to develop projects and elaborate solutions.

The above mentioned dynamic generates *"learners-centered communities"*, conceived as open learning networks fostering diversity and autonomy, as illustrated in Fig. 1.4.

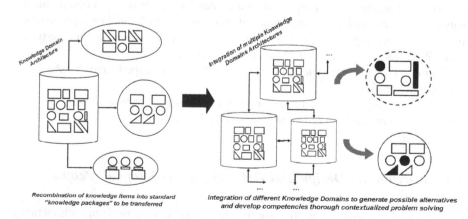

Recombination of knowledge items into standard   Integration of different Knowledge Domains to generate possible alternatives
"knowledge packages" to be transferred   and develop competencies thorough contextualized problem solving

Fig. 1.3 The shift in curriculum architecture

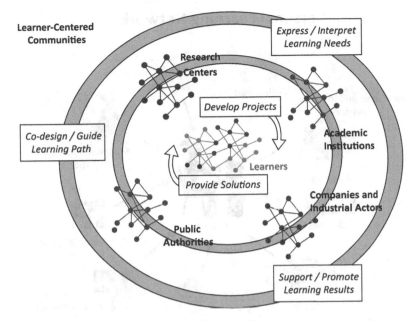

Fig. 1.4 Learners-centered communities' architecture

At micro-level, within the community, each learner has his/her personal learning network constituted by resources, people, knowledge assets, technological platforms and social relationships that participate to his/her learning process and activities. Figure 1.5 provides an example of a personal learning network.

Within these communities, it's fundamental to adopt an effective strategy for curricula delivery. This means that learning designers have to select a right mixture of learning methods to guarantee an active involvement of learners and high retention rate of learning process (Harris 2001). Figure 1.6 gives some insights about this issue.

An operational approach to follow for reaching high retention rates can be the *"3P-Learning approach"*, consisting in the organization of the entire learning experience around three main challenges:

- Problem resolution.
- Project development.
- Process execution.

The "3P-Learning approach" guarantees the *responsibility* of learners in self organizing their learning pattern, as well as the *interdisciplinarity* in the knowledge/learning bases.

Actually, *problem resolution* is basically grounded on an inquiry-based behaviour of learners, who have to discover various scenarios and alternatives to formulate a possible solution to the problem. Often, the final result cannot be foreseen, because it is strongly related to the competencies, creativity and entrepreneurial spirit of each learner.

Personal Learning Network

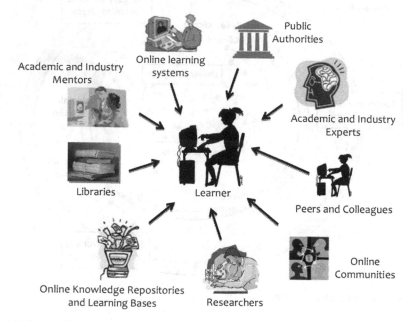

Fig. 1.5 Personal learning network

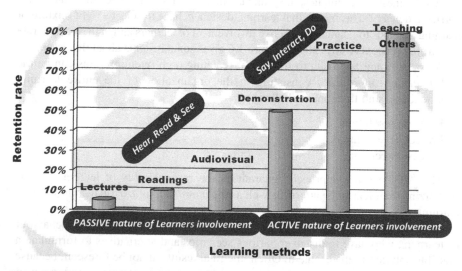

Fig. 1.6 Effective learning delivery methods

Project development consists in the execution of a predefined task, previously conceived and planned. Normally, the final result is compatible with the requested requirements, and consequently it can be objectively evaluated according to a standard list of parameters and standards.

Process execution gives a more dynamic vision to the learning process. Learners are constantly engaged to transform inputs into outputs, to coordinate activities, to use resources, to respect guidelines and rules, to manage people and to organize technical, financial and intangible assets for generating valuable outputs. During this process, they have to choose the right methods, equipments and infrastructures, as well as to adopt a suitable measurement system and effective key performance indicators (KPI) for controlling and monitoring the entire process.

The enabling configuration of the learning environments implementing the "3P-learning approach" is represented by the *"incubator"*, in which curricula are organized around business, organizational, strategic and technological processes, and where people are actively involved in real projects to solve challenging problems. Actually, the integrated mix of the 3P learning approach's components allow to "incubate" new talented people, characterized by vertical knowledge and competencies, as well as by transversal skills, attitudes and individual capabilities. Definitively, these learning environments operate as "incubators" of Π-shaped professionals.

3 Innovating Learning Processes Through the Open Networked "i-Learning" Model: Key Characteristics and Guidelines

This section provides an attempt to propose a new model around which to design effective learning experiences that move from the needs and observations discussed above, referring primarily to the changes happening in ICT, management and society.

Actually, since learning is a complex process involving all the aspects and dimensions of a person, and since today learning reveals to be the most strategic process within the organizations, the proposed model aims to activate a continuous debate on methodologies, strategies and tools focused on experimenting innovation in learning processes, both at individual and at community or organizational level.

The need to innovate learning processes is considered as an urgency from top managers, executives and universities' presidents. It represents a hot topic in management, in humanities, in technology, in engineering contexts. This section contributes to operationalize the innovation process at learning level, through the proposition of a *"learning incubator"*, by providing a process-based perspective and a technology-based perspective, as well as some operational guidelines to implement it.

In this context, a "learning incubator" can be conceived and interpreted as a stimulating, creative, experimenting, exploratory, rigorous, opened and empowering milieu of experiential knowledge, workplace applications, collaborative processes and enabling technologies supporting competency development and lifelong learning processes (Vest 2006).

The learning incubator finds its inspiration in the principle of *"open innovation"* (Chesbrough 2003). Actually, the value can be generated through the embedding of external sources of knowledge or innovation is bigger and more valuable than the value produced by the single organization itself. The same situation happens when an organization decides to make public the know-how it develops: the quantity and the quality of the opportunities to exploit the value embedded in that "innovation" increases sensibly according to the level of openness of the entire system.

Besides openness, learning incubator embeds also the *networking* perspective. So, it drives fully human capital development by investigating and addressing two fundamental dimensions: (a) the inter-organizational collaboration and the interdisciplinary approach in designing learning bases and knowledge architectures, and (b) the analysis of the knowledge flows and patterns of interaction happening in communities, and their impact on individual and collective learning networks.

On these assumptions, the "learning incubator" tries to contextualize the principle and the meaning of the openness in the learning context, leveraging on five key pillars (Secundo et al. 2009b):

- Number and participation level of stakeholders involved in designing and delivering the learning experience.
- Richness of internal and external knowledge sources used to feed the learning process.
- Intensity of the knowledge sharing processes amongst learners and mentors/tutors.
- Level of integration of theoretical concepts with concrete and real life problems.
- Level of integrability of the technological environment with external systems.

It can be conceived as an open "space" in which people can learn and interact with challenges, problems, ideas and inspirations; in which they can cultivate and nurture curiosity, passion, motivation, engagement and dreams, and where they can practice actively ICT and Internet-based services.

The model is inspired to the connectivism theory (Siemens 2004; Ally 2008), that overcomes traditional theories like behaviorism (Skinner 1953), cognitivism (Bruner 1966) and constructivism (Dewey 1966; Piaget 1977; Vygotskii 1978).

Actually, behaviourism, initially developed by John Watson in early 1900 (Watson 1913), is based on the metaphor of the "transfer" (Baets and Van der Linden 2003), in which teacher transmits knowledge to learners through mechanisms based on stimulus and rewards. Learners assume a passive role; they act as recipients of knowledge to be filled in, with no interactions amongst them and with the teachers, with a pre-defined set of results that personally have to reach.

Around the mid of 1950s, cognitivism theory matured as evolution of behaviorism. It valorises learners' capacities and intelligence, who create relationships among knowledge concepts and personal experiences. Learning happens not automatically, but it is related to the learner's specific individualities.

This new approach is further developed by the constructivism theory (early 1980) that considers learner as an active participant of the learning process, including also the context in which he operates and the collaborations he cultivates. So, accordingly, learning is the result of a knowledge sharing process amongst all the participants, involving also the elements of the context in which it happens and the collaborations existing among all the participants.

Ultimately, connectivism integrates principles explored by network, complexity and self-organization theories. According to this theory, learning is a process that occurs within nebulous environments of shifting core elements, not entirely under the control of the individual. Connections with knowledge sources and specialized network of experts (independently if they are internal or external) become a source of knowledge, complementing individual learning process. Connectivism is based on the metaphor of the travel (Baets and Van der Linden 2003), in which teacher is an expert guide who guides students through an unknown terrain to explore, by providing them the tools and techniques to go on, and by stimulating them to be more "entrepreneurial" in their learning experiences.

Definitively, the learning incubator wants to overcome current learning environments traditionally characterized by static curricula based on high-specialized and "on-the-shelf" courses, theory-based examination, fixed space and equipment, close to external "contamination", teaching approach based on knowledge transfer, deep separation between education and research, rare context-oriented applications, and a marginal role and limited usage of ICT and Internet. In this sense, the proposal constitutes a challenge mainly for today's universities and business schools that need to be re-thought and re-invented if they want to play a primary role in creating human capital and professionals able to activate innovation and value generating processes in the twenty-first century economy.

In this perspective, it is necessary to evolve towards open, motivating, dynamic and networked learning environments enabling knowledge acquisition and application, (virtual) participation and actions in interdisciplinary, multi-sector, multicultural, even multinational teams addressing challenging problems and opportunities. The radical mindset into the learning incubator model can represent an effective answer to the urgent challenges of rapid competence obsolescence and exponential knowledge growth and, at the same time, to the pressing need to boost innovation for competitiveness and value creation.

This (r)evolution is aligned to Gibbon's approach to knowledge production based on transition from *Mode 1* to *Mode 2* (Gibbons et al. 1994). The approach concerns the following issues:

- What knowledge is produced.
- Who are the actors that produce knowledge.
- How knowledge is produced and how the involved actors are organized.

- The context where knowledge is produced.
- The mechanisms that control the quality of what is produced.

Specifically, Mode 1 of knowledge production is characterized by the hegemony of theoretical approach having low interaction with applicative contexts, a limited attention to problems, no exchanges with community of experts (scientists and academicians), a high focus on a single discipline, often based on individual studies, homogeneity of the application contexts, self-referential behaviours, hierarchical approach to organize the activities, quality control based on peer evaluation, low impact of social accountability.

On the contrary, Mode 2 of knowledge production considers that problems are not restricted to a discipline or a group of disciplines (multi-disciplinary), they are interdisciplinary, highly linked to real applicative contexts, proposed by a group of stakeholders interested in its solution and potential impacts. Moreover, the work is carried out in non-hierarchical, heterogeneous and flexible organizational forms, with a collaborative style and a close interaction to many actors. Besides, the production of knowledge becomes more socially accountable, and it utilizes a wide range of criteria and a multi-stakeholders perspective to implement quality control.

Table 1.2 shows the main difference between Mode 1 and Mode 2 of knowledge production.

The attempt pursued in this book goes also in the direction to add another column to the above table. Specifically, we can imagine a *Mode 3* of knowledge production in which two dimensions are mainly stressed: (a) the role of stakeholders in defining the problems, in contributing actively to carry out the activities, and in evaluating the benefits of the results; (b) the approach adopted by every "knowledge worker/producer", at every level, that is characterized mainly by a bottom up behaviour, rather than a top down style, in order to leave more space and time to creativity, ideas, inventiveness, and collective intelligence, whose results could generate new valuable opportunities to explore and to exploit.

Actually, the model of learning incubator tries to implement a mixture of Mode 2 and Mode 3 of knowledge production. It realizes a shift from the traditional

Table 1.2 Mode 1 and Mode 2 of knowledge production

Mode 1	Mode 2
Theoretical approach with low interaction with applicative contexts	Practical approach and high interaction with real contexts and stakeholders
Limited problems proposed and solved by a specific community	Complex problems proposed and solved in the context of applications and through the collaboration of different communities
Disciplinary approach	Interdisciplinary approach
Hierarchical approach to organize the activities	Non-hierarchical, heterogeneous and flexible organization of work
Quality control based on peer evaluation	Wide range of criteria and a multi-stakeholders perspective
Low impact of social accountability	High social accountability

"client-server" perspective based on broadcast, closed and static knowledge transfer processes, to a collaborative-distributed model based on *openness* (blurred boundaries), *peering* (no hierarchical relationships), *sharing* (collective intelligence to reduce complexity), *diversity* (interdisciplinarity of contents and multi-agent approach), and individualization (personalized learning experience).

Table 1.3 presents the paradigm shift characterizing the learning incubator model, organizing each "item of change" in seven main categories (Romano 2008):

Table 1.3 The paradigm shift characterizing the learning incubator model

Category	Item	From	To
Actors	Main actor	Teacher	Network of peers (mentors, learners, tutors, experts, researchers, testimonials, institutional representatives)
	Target	Students	Knowledge workers, knowledge producers and public/private stakeholders
Strategy	Approach	Theory before practice	Integration of theory and practice (problems, projects, processes, cases)
	Pedagogy	Knowledge transfer	Competence development
	Typology of interaction	Unidirectional (teacher vs student)	Collaborative (network of peers)
	Style	Top-down	Bottom-up
Curriculum	Knowledge	Discipline-based/conceptual knowledge	Interdisciplinary/experiential knowledge
	Architecture	Well-structured, static and domain-specific	Hyperlinked, dynamic and multi-domains
	Resources	Books, and rarely PC	Digital library, e-books, wikis and blogs, web repositories, open courseware, and books
Technology	Role of technology	Marginal	Pervasive and flexible, with the usage of interactive tools, and audio-video real time systems.
Metrics	Evaluation and assessment	Individual theory-based examination	Collaborative and group-based results/solutions
Space	Place	Closed classroom	Laboratories, open community and physical/virtual/mental space
	Context	Ambiguous and general	Well defined and workplace-oriented
	Scope	Local	Global
Time	Frequency	Fixed and scheduled, push	On demand, pull
	Duration	Limited	Unlimited and lifelong

The model of the learning incubator is following presented, by highlighting the *process-based perspective* and the *technology-based perspective*

- *Actors*, that represents the dimension associated both to the real animators of the learning experience, and to its main target.
- *Strategy*, that characterizes the processes and the dynamic of the learning practice.
- *Curriculum*, that describes the knowledge architecture feeding the learning experience.
- *Technology*, that illustrates the ICT-based tools and their role in the learning system.
- *Metrics*, that highlights the assessment procedure and principles to measure learning effectiveness and results.
- *Space*, that gives both a physical and a virtual (mental) state to the learning environment.
- *Time*, that presents the temporal features of the learning activities.

3.1   The Process-Based Perspective

The process-based perspective highlights the dynamic view of the incubator, emphasizing the approaches and strategies mainly used to activate the individual/collaborative learning experience. The main processes can be synthesized in the following ones (Garvin 1993; Leonard-Barton 1992):

- *Problem Solving.* Usually, problems cut right across the borders of any subject matter or discipline, so promoting an interdisciplinary approach to learning. As much complex a problem is, as much "effective" the learning process reveals in terms of specific competencies, knowledge and skills developed and acquired by the learner. In problem solving process, egalitarianism and mutual respect represent two fundamental values, since they favour all the individuals to contribute to the joint experience, without any fear to express their own ideas. Finally, a sense of "urgency", generated through some forms of external pressure, sustain the problem solving process.
- *Internal and External Knowledge Integration.* Apprenticeship and continuous learning are the energy for feeding the entire process. Combination and integration of experiences, best practices, lesson learned, publications and techniques belonging to different disciplines, mixed with cross-industry perspectives favour the creation of new (and often unexpected) connections that envision innovative solutions to existing problems.
- *Experimentation and Innovation.* Bright, enthusiastic and motivated people, with a positive attitude toward risk, high skilled and attracted by continuous innovation, represent the main driver to promise a value generating solutions. Thinking through new perspectives and breaking existent patterns and structures generate a climate favourable to experimentation and innovation. Typically, ongoing programs and demonstration projects contribute to perform a series of small experiments for reaching incremental gains and to experiment more complex initiatives whose results generate big and pervasive changes.

– *Knowledge Transferring and Application.* Value is not so much related to the source of the knowledge itself, but mainly in its usefulness in the real life application and in activating new and faster learning processes. Reciprocal trust amongst the actors and openness toward external stakeholders to share knowledge play a strategic role in activating these exchanges for creating (and learning) collaboratively.

– *Communication.* Encouraging listening to each other, exploring jointly new concepts and paradigms, promoting and valorizing ethical behaviors, creating connections amongst existing and/or new inputs and/or outputs, creating and sharing a common vision, etc … all these elements improve and strengthen incubator's learning process, making them more effective.

The activation of the above mentioned processes happens through a cycle of four main steps, referable to the *Kolb's cycle* (Kolb 1984).

The first step named *"Concrete Experience"* involves learners in an active exploration of the (simulated) reality, in which they focus their perception and attention to what they see and to how they react. Simulators, games, laboratories and on field activities are the most common tools used for this step.

Then, *"Reflective Observation"* step aims to deepen the exact meaning and description of the concepts and the observed reality. Individual study and collective discussions contribute to clarify concepts and stylized facts. Readings, observations and brainstorming are the most common tools used for this step.

The third step is the *"Abstract Conceptualization"* and it is focused on developing capabilities to approach systematically complex problems and to activate a logic path conducting to the elaboration of possible alternatives. Learners are involved in understanding and applying theories, models and diagrams useful to represent and describe logically several scenarios and problem statements. Lectures, articles, books, theories, models and diagrams are the most common tools used for this step.

Finally, the *"Active Experimentation"* step aims to design, apply and experiment the elaborated alternatives, observing the on going and the final results, possible malfunctioning and improvement points, in the final perspective to choose the most valuable solution. Simulators, laboratories and real projects are the most common tools used for this step.

Figure 1.7 provides a systemic view of the process-based perspective of the incubator.

The process-based perspective of the incubator implements the learning approaches and strategies adopted during the design, delivery and assessment phases of the entire learning experience.

Actually, the processes and the cycle in Fig. 1.7 contribute to operationalize several learning approaches and strategies, such as inquiry learning, problem-based learning, project-based learning, process-based learning and case-based learning. These strategies promote interactions and communication between faculty and learners, but also they allow people to understand real contexts and to deepen the different observed aspects, in the final perspective to develop competencies and to create new value.

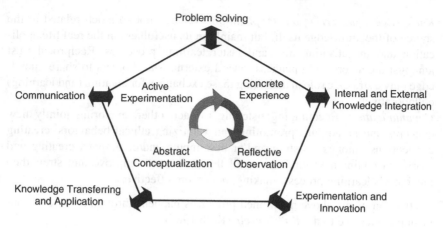

Fig. 1.7 A systemic view of the process-based perspective of the incubator

3.2 The Technological-Based Perspective

Technology represents just a mean to reach the goal; it is not the end itself. Today technological infrastructure plays the same role of the paper and pencil in the twentieth century; it behaves as an enabler of the learning processes since it creates virtuous connections among working, learning and innovation. The technological-based perspective allows to create effective links amongst the strategic resources of the learning incubator:

- A set of distributed services for competency management, content management and community management, integrated by an interactive dashboard for monitoring the learning dynamics.
- An interactive and dynamic knowledge base made up of physical contents and digital resources.
- Real and virtual laboratories, connected each other through a networked architecture.
- A portfolio of relationships with several typologies of actors (learners, mentors, academic and business testimonials, experts, institutional representatives, etc.).

New devices like mobile tools, 3D and ambient intelligence systems complement the components of the learning microcosm.

These resources are activated and utilized by single learners or collaborative communities of learners through the definition of a set of personal learning networks (PLN) constituted by services belonging to:

- *Virtual Learning Systems*, mainly used for competency management process.
- *Knowledge Management Systems*, mainly used for content management process.

– *Collaborative Working Systems*, mainly used for community management process.

Through their own PLN, people can build and nurture relationships between individuals for mutual learning. In PLN people can exchange feedback, insights, documentation, contacts, ideas and business opportunities. Reciprocity and mutual trust enrich all the involved parties, making more valuable the single participation (Digenti 1999).

Each PLN operates (uses/feeds) on a dynamic knowledge base integrating different disciplines. Each knowledge item is considered as an independent (multimedia) resource, with multiple possibilities to be linked to other (internal/external) resources. Symbolically, each item can be positioned in a five-dimensional space characterized by the following dimensions: (a) *concepts*, representing the basic unit of the entire knowledge architecture; (b) *cases*, representing real applications, best/worst practices, experiences and codified know how from which extracting strategic and operational guidelines; (c) *competencies*, that reflect the ability and the skills to perform effectively a job or a task; (d) *activities*, that inspire the entire learning experience through the involvement of learners in projects dynamics; (e) *problems*, the real context of the learning incubator, in which different disciplines, different backgrounds and complementary expertise interact each other to design and implement a real solution.

The five-dimensional organization of the space allows to identify, extract, insert or compose complex knowledge resources according to a specific need, for example a competence to fulfill, or a problem to solve, or an activity to perform, or a case to analyze, or a concept to deepen. The flexibility of this organization allows to fulfill several learning approaches such as problem-based learning, project-based learning, process-based learning, case-based learning and curricula-based learning. In any case, each learning experience based on this dynamic and interactive knowledge base introduces modifications and updates both at competence level and at conceptual level.

Considering the above mentioned service platforms, the Virtual Learning System ensures an effective management of competencies and skills of learners participating to the incubator. Managing the right mix between knowledge and experience, monitoring progresses of competence profiles and identifying development plans both at individual and organizational levels represent key features of virtual learning systems. This implies also defining an appropriate portfolio of skills, attitudes and knowledge required for the specific context in which those competencies have to be applied. Also the policies to create project teams are impacted, such as the identification of people with the necessary profile and expertise requested to perform a specific task. An effective monitoring system is necessary to point out emergency situations and to recommend actions for fulfilling competence gaps. Specific tools like simulators, case base reasoning systems or user-friendly authoring tools enrich the service offerings and give more chances to practice knowledge and skills.

As for the Knowledge Management System, it guarantees a correct management of the life cycle of each piece of (multimedia/interactive) content stored in the knowledge base. Distributed authoring tools and multiple (internal and external) sources ensure always-on processes of knowledge identification and collection, indexing and classification, and then knowledge distribution and application. Content management services ensure an effective execution of distributed work-flow processes. The adoption of reasoning methods and artificial intelligence techniques to create a semantic layer on different knowledge sources (e.g. electronic libraries, case studies repositories, journals directory, e-books, technical reports), makes more effective knowledge retrieval processes. Besides, the usage of interactive knowledge maps and customizable (semantic) search engines contribute to make more user-friendly the knowledge extraction.

Finally, as for the Collaborative Working System, it enables to create and nurture (virtual) learning communities, conceived as places in which learning processes occur, knowledge exchanges happen, new ideas arise, new products and services are designed, new projects are developed, and individual and organizational growth can take place. At this purpose, collaborative design tools, group decision support systems, integrated by multimedia collaboration suites, project management suites and social computing spaces support the interactions within the community and among different communities. Monitoring of these interactions and relationships is guarantee by Social Networking Analysis (SNA) tools that provide interesting suggestions and feedback to enhance quality and effectiveness of decision making processes.

Figure 1.8 provides an integrated view of a generic PLN activated by the incubator, in which services and tools interact each other, and with the contents stored in the five-dimensions hyper-textual knowledge base.

The figure highlights also the role of two fundamental gateways: one to guarantee external connections with other Internet/Extranet/Intranet services, and one to ensure connection with tools and services available in the laboratories in which practicing learning and knowledge.

Based on this technological perspective, learning incubator can be represented as an ecosystem of Personal Learning Networks, generating virtuous interactions among services, people, contents and technologies.

3.3 Operational Guidelines

Table 1.3 illustrated above shown the paradigm shift characterizing the learning incubator model. To make operational this shift, it is necessary to formulate a set of practical guidelines that sustain its implementation. Specifically, these guidelines aim to support learning systems engineers in designing effective learning environment. To be more practical and mission-oriented, Tables 1.4–1.10 present the guidelines organized according to the dimension along which implementing the shift.

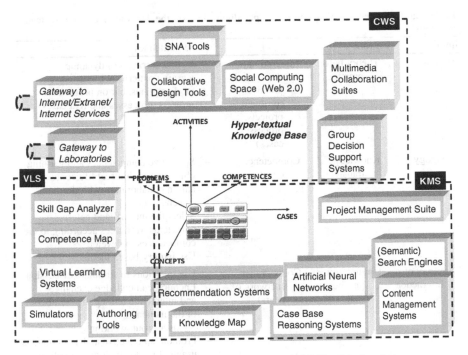

Fig. 1.8 An integrated view of the personal learning network (PLN) of the incubator

Table 1.4 Guidelines implementing the paradigm shift of the learning incubator (category "Actors")

Item	From	To	Some guidelines
Main actor	Teacher	Network of peers (mentors, learners, tutors, experts, researchers, testimonials, institutional representatives)	– Highlight the need of a radical change in teachers' and learners' behavior – Involve the (heterogeneous) actors in a joint work for designing the learning experience; – Promote dialogue, collaboration and trust, reciprocal growth
Target	Students	Knowledge workers, knowledge producers and public/private stakeholders	– Promote learning experiences based on specific company's needs, and associating also students – Organize interactive meetings among (young) students and adults to debate on new required competencies, skills and attitudes deriving from the emerging global and complex scenarios

Table 1.5 Guidelines implementing the paradigm shift of the learning incubator (category "Strategy")

Item	From	To	Some guidelines
Approach	Theory before practice	Integration of theory and practice (problems, projects, processes, cases)	– Define curricula as dynamic learning patterns not focused on disciplines, but on problems, projects, processes and real cases
Pedagogy	Knowledge transfer	Competence development	– Specialize competences and learning objectives within real life contexts, and in collaboration with the stakeholders – Select the internal and external knowledge resources according to the competences to develop – Use inquiry-based methods
Typology of Interaction	Unidirectional (teacher vs student)	Collaborative (network of peers)	– Use questions to stimulate discussion – Encourage knowledge exchanges and interaction among the members of the incubator – Sponsor group working – Promote an effective and a continuous usage of the technological platforms supporting communication and exchanges
Style	Top-down	Bottom-up	– Reserve time for personal deepening and study, exploiting personal curiosities and interests – Encourage periodic meetings and exchanges with colleagues, also of different areas and disciplines, to explore the feasibility of new ideas

Table 1.6 Guidelines implementing the paradigm shift of the learning incubator (category "Curriculum")

Item	From	To	Some guidelines
Knowledge	Discipline-based/ conceptual knowledge	Interdisciplinary/ experiential knowledge	– Highlight the importance of the contribution of different disciplines during the problem analysis and problem solving – Alternate seminal sessions with on field experience, testimonies, demonstrations and hands-on sessions

(continued)

Table 1.6 (continued)

Item	From	To	Some guidelines
Architecture	Well-structured, static and domain-specific	Hyperlinked, dynamic and multi-domains	– Organize contents by merging internal and external knowledge sources – Mixing different typologies of contents (paper based and electronic; books and papers; newspaper and web pages; text and movie; etc)
Resources	Books, and rarely PC	Digital library, e-books, wikis and blogs, web repositories, open courseware, and books	– Sensitize to use electronic resources available within digital libraries – Encourage the usage of web based tools to access to information and people – Sustain and coach people who adopt heterogeneous devices to perform their tasks

Table 1.7 Guidelines implementing the paradigm shift of the learning incubator (category "Technology")

Item	From	To	Some guidelines
Role of Technology	Marginal	Pervasive and flexible, with the usage of interactive tools, and audio–video real time systems.	– Focus on "user experience" and "simplicity" during the design of the technological solutions – Think in terms of needs and services, not in terms of technological components – Hide complexity of the technological assets – Maximize reuse strategy and adopt a service oriented approach – Encourage networking approach with existing available service providers and platforms – Use open laboratories to carry on learning activities

Table 1.8 Guidelines implementing the paradigm shift of the learning incubator (category "Metrics")

Item	From	To	Some guidelines
Evaluation and assessment	Individual theory-based examination	Collaborative and group-based results/solutions	– Organize plenary sessions with stakeholders to discuss the produced outcomes – Make hypothesis on how to valorize the obtained outcomes

Table 1.9 Guidelines implementing the paradigm shift of the learning incubator (category "Space")

Item	From	To	Some guidelines
Place	Closed classroom	Laboratories, open community and physical/virtual/ mental space	– Plan frequently virtual meetings and web conferences to be integrated with face-to-face sessions – Promote hands-on sessions, building of prototypes and experimentations – Encourage (individual/collective) reflection and internalization of knowledge
Context	Ambiguous and general	Well defined and workplace-oriented	– Create learning experiences around specific needs of stakeholders – Alternate delivery of concepts with application to real life settings
Scope	Local	Global	– Invite foreign people to animate the learning sessions – Alternate seminars in different languages, also using multimedia sources – Create a multicultural and international environment, by preserving specific traditions and languages through ad-hoc initiatives

Table 1.10 Guidelines implementing the paradigm shift of the learning incubator (category "Time")

Item	From	To	Some guidelines
Frequency	Fixed and scheduled, push	On demand, pull	– Design and offer just in time learning "pills" mapped to granular needs, problems or objectives
Duration	Limited	Unlimited and lifelong	– Sensitize people on the value generated by knowledge application – Highlight the overlapping between work and learning in the perspective of innovation – Develop and experiment "learning to learn" attitudes and abilities

4 Open Networked "i-Learning" Radar

Extracting from the previous section the main "messages" that have been presented and discussed, that characterize the recent changes in technology, management and society/workplace, here six main keywords are introduced to design, implement, delivery and monitor a learning experience contextualized in the open learning incubator. These six keywords constitute the main dimensions through which representing – in an intuitive form – the innovation in learning process:

- Interdisciplinarity;
- Interactivity;
- Internetworking;
- Individualization;
- Immediacy;
- Interoperability.

The full comprehension of these keywords and the capability to operationalize and contextualize their meaning in the workplace and in experimental academic courses, will stimulate learners, mentors, tutors and the entire organization (private or public) to envision the future of the learning process.

Each of the six dimensions is presented through a multi-dimensional perspective: a technological point of view, a managerial interpretation and a social aspect. This choice wants to highlight the multi-faceted impact on the learning dimension. Actually, a contextualization of each dimension to the learning process is provided, to deepen and clarify the real meaning, according to the proposed open networked i-learning model.

4.1   Interdisciplinarity

"We are not students of some subject matter, but students of problems. And problems may cut right across the borders of any subject matter or discipline."

(Popper 1963)

This definition of interdisciplinarity given by Karl Popper provides a clear meaning of this word, and above all it highlights the importance of the interdisciplinary approach to face complex challenges. It is not matter of merging different disciplines that contribute and collaborate to give different perspectives on a single phenomenon; interdisciplinarity overcomes the barriers of single autonomous and separate disciplines, by promoting a new approach that integrates the single knowledge-based disciplines to create a new complex and systemic model to interpret the complex phenomenon. Normally, the final outcome is sensibly different and more valuable of the sum of the single discipline-based contributions.

Often, there is a sort of confusion among *multi-disciplinarity*, *cross-disciplinarity* and *inter-disciplinarity*.

With a multi-disciplinary approach, it is possible to "activate" distinct disciplines that give different perspectives on a single problem. Each discipline does not overlap with other disciplines, but it coexists and it contribute with a partial interpretation of the phenomenon.

In a cross-disciplinary approach, each discipline is seen as a black-box, and other disciplines can use it to interpret other phenomena. No strong cooperation among experts of different disciplines exists.

In an inter-disciplinary approach, different expert of different disciplines interact each other, exchange reciprocal knowledge, create together new knowledge, and each single expertise becomes part of a more complex and holistic vision. It's like a concert of classic music: each instrument can play alone, but the result of the entire orchestra is richer, more valuable, more complete, and it opens new spaces for creating new and exciting results.

In technology, interdisciplinarity is at the basis of the on going process of technological convergence that is interesting biotechnologies, nanotechnologies, materials technologies, and information and communication technologies (Silberglitt et al. 2006). This process is generating completely new industries that will be always more profitable and able to revolutionize traditional competitive dynamics. Two examples of this trend are the smart fabrics and textiles, and the personalized medicine and therapies. These two "simple" examples give immediately the huge potential incorporated in the interdisciplinary approach to the technologies.

The interdisciplinary approach reveals its usefulness also in management field, where it allows to make more effective the decision making process, developed also in a collaborative way. Also in social aspects, interdisciplinarity plays an important role since it stimulates curiosity in individuals and collaboration among groups.

After these considerations, learning processes should consider the interdisciplinarity as one of the most important pillar on which basing the radical innovation process, if it wants to develop new professional profiles (such T-shaped or Π-shaped people) that are able to face the complex challenges of the next decades.

4.2   Interactivity

Conceived as highly responsive behavior adopted by people or machines, interactivity is a key dimension inspiring the innovation process at learning level.

Typically used in ICT industry to represent amazing interfaces, attractive software applications and nice-looking digital contents, interactivity characterizes also the managerial style. Actually, interactive management highlights that effective actions to solve complex situations require multiple perspectives of problem analysis, and continuous discussion and sharing of knowledge and experiences to be carried out in a collaborative environment. Capacity to adopt an interactive management style helps organization to activate effective organizational knowledge creation processes, strongly aligned to strategic business choices. Finally, interactivity expresses also an important dimension of social behavior. The explosion of virtual communities and social networking spaces is an indicator of the individuals' need to contact and communicate with other people. Actually, searching for other people, often unknown but with a similar profile of interests, represents an interesting social phenomenon that offer new opportunities to communicate, to discuss, to learn.

Definitively, interactivity can be considered as a fundamental aspect of learning process innovation. It encompasses the dynamicity in the usage of ICT and Internet-based tools, and the exploration of distributed digital content repositories and services. Besides, interactivity embraces also the presence of a collaborative community of people (and stakeholders), open to dialogue and novelty, and interested in sharing and discussing valuable ideas. Dynamic patterns built on the basis of learner's profile enhance the dynamicity level of the whole learning experience.

4.3   Internetworking

A word that embeds the concept of the "network", projecting it both in the technological perspective and in the organizational and social environment. From the technological side, it focuses on the Internet as a general purpose technology enabling every actions and processes (Internet-working). More interesting is the management interpretation of this word; it highlights the emerging paradigm of the *"extended enterprise"* through the integration and the collaboration among different networks of actors and organizations (inter-networking).

Actually, shifts from centralization to decentralization and from hierarchies to networks underline the increasing of organizational connectivity level. The explosion of networking process with other organizations through alliances, partnerships and outsourcing emphasizes the disintegration of organizational barriers and the creation of open business communities where single actors interact each other to design and implement win–win business models.

At learning level, internetworking illustrates from one side the heterogeneity of participants and from the other side the strategic role of the Internet as the underpinning infrastructure enabling distributed and collaborative environments. As for the first issue (heterogeneity of participants), the need to innovate learning dynamics calls for a rethinking of the organization's boundaries, in order to include all the relevant stakeholders. This contributes to add more value to the traditional learning process. Actually, the final development of the competencies in single participants is not the unique final aim; it is just a mean through which creating new value for a larger number of stakeholders.

As for the second issue (Internet as the underpinning infrastructure enabling distributed and collaborative environments), there is no doubt that today's learning processes benefit from technological applications and infrastructures. Internet constitutes the "social" highway through which data, contents, knowledge and experiences flow. Low accessing cost, wide diffusion and ubiquitous access allow an "always-on" presence on the net, so favoring collaboration among all the participants.

4.4   Individualization

Individual was, is and will be always the basic fundamental pillar of the learning process. Individualization represents an important dimension to consider when offering a product or a service; it represents a key driver to personalize and make unique a user's experience.

From the technological perspective, individualization and customization constitute the "killer" application to succeed. They represent the phase in which individual participate actively in the design and production of products and services, so generating sometimes unique outcomes. Recommendation systems and personal agents perform this activity, so adding new value to the entire process, product or service.

In management, it highlights a very important dimension of the organization, linked to the key role played by individuals. At this purpose, Ghoshal and Bartlett in their volume *"The Individualized Corporation"* reveal the emergence of a different management philosophy based on the power of the individual's unique talents and skills as the driver of value creation in the company, as well as on the importance of individuality in management practices (Ghoshal and Bartlett 1999).

In the learning field, it is necessary to balance the interests of single individual with the mission of the organization, the individual motivation to develop new competencies with the organizational constraints to invest in human capital development strategies, the expectation of the individual in his own career development with the organizational chart. A right mix among learning services, learning contents and learning technologies, joint to a right balance between individual learning goals and organizational business goals, represent the scenario in which a learning experience carries out.

Another dimension to take in consideration is the relationship between individual learning dynamics and community-based interactions. Actually, by searching, reading and interpreting information, learners live their experience in their personal environments, supported by their personal devices, agents, filtering systems and maybe also by their personal programs. This leads to the creation of a personalization level, immersed in a community-based environment, which helps to enforce both individual and collaborative learning dynamics.

4.5 Immediacy

Interpreted as synonym of readiness, immediacy is another pillar of the innovation process at learning level.

It indicates rapidity in actions; it is an expression of the instantaneous feedback given by a person or a system. At social level, immediacy is a characteristic of real-time experience; people expect direct and prompt messages to their stimuli.

Continuous cycles of fast responding events generate high level of complexity in management practices. Decision making processes are part of a continuous adaptive strategy, coherent with internal and external changes, and always in motion since it results from a collaborative process of people's and systems' feedbacks.

At learning level, immediacy is on the basis of the "just in time" paradigm, that ensures competency development when and where knowledge workers need them. Rather than attending for hours the traditional classroom training, usually people prefer and choose to access directly just to the information they need to solve problems, to perform specific tasks or to update their skills quickly. At this purpose, *"learning pills"* can be distributed or accessed through several devices, and people learn in their workplace. So, the matured experiential knowledge becomes part of the people's knowledge background. Immediacy favors *informal learning*, in the sense that the formal process is not structured or organized (referring to specific learning objectives, time slots or learning support) and usually does not lead to any kind of certificate; it is often unintentionally, happening in daily life, at work, within family life or on leisure time. Immediacy contributes also to develop in learners reactive and proactive attitudes, enhancing their motivation since they are put in the conditions to answer and interact in real time to the stimuli generated by other people or by external systems and events.

4.6 Interoperability

Interoperability refers to the ability of diverse systems (organizations, or individuals, or technological platforms) to work together, to inter-operate. Usually, depending on the typology of the relationships existing among the diverse systems and on its management tools, performance of the entire system is affected.

In management, interoperability can be interpreted as an expression of the attitude of the organization to collaborate with other partners; it's a sort of measure of the opening degree of the organization. Interoperability is a founding principle of the *"extended enterprise"* paradigm: from one side it refers to the challenges of the global coordination and controls of disintegrated supply chains in a complex environment (design, manufacturing, procurement, distribution, service, upgrade, and disposal); from the other side, it refers directly to the technological infrastructures and standards regulating its implementation (e-business systems, transaction standards, "securization" of the knowledge accesses and exchanges, etc.).

In the learning perspective, interoperability mostly refers to the possibility to integrate existing services and contents, so creating a more attractive environment facilitating the learning processes. Since learning is a transversal "practice" that impacts on many organizational units, and it gives a fundamental support in decision making process and in implementing the business strategy, it requires a strong support from existing knowledge assets and technological infrastructure. Interoperability in learning means cooperation among technological systems, integration of contents and collaboration among people.

These six dimensions can be qualitatively measured and plotted in a radar graph, like the one illustrated in Fig. 1.9, in order to have immediately the perception about the innovation characterizing the design or delivery phases of a learning experience.

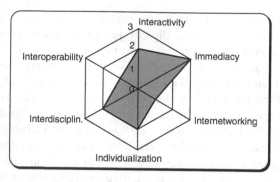

Fig. 1.9 An example of the "i-Learning" radar

5 Discussion and Conclusions

This first chapter constitutes an attempt to propose a strategic and an operational model enabling open networked i-learning processes, in the perspective to innovate the human capital development processes within the organizations.

Actually, the proposed model aims to provide an answer to the challenges that world wide organizations have to face today in a global competitive scenario. The unique lever at their disposal is represented by the human capital, the most strategic resource strongly subjected to obsolescence phenomenon that impacts on professionals' competency profiles. Thus, developing new knowledge, competencies and skills, and supporting individuals in their self learning processes are two crucial processes within organizations that must be stimulated and cultivated. In this perspective, the model is also presented as a framework through which developing new professional profiles, like T-shaped and Π-shaped, that, from one side, allow to reach a more effective and efficient result and, from the other side, they can activate endogenous processes of self-development and lifelong learning, fundamental processes for people and organizations who want to remain competitive and to create new value.

But, how to implement systematically this strategy, ensuring high level of effectiveness? The model proposed in this chapter, completed by the operational guidelines and the "i-Learning Radar", aims to contribute in formulating an answer to this question.

References

Ally M (2008) Foundations of Educational Theory for Online Learning. In: Anderson T and Elloumi F (Eds.) The Theory and Practice of Online Learning. Athabasca University. Canada
Afuah A and Tucci C L (2003) Internet Business Models and Strategies. McGraw-Hill. New York
Anderson C (2006) The Long Tail. Hyperion. New York

Baets W and Van der Linden G (2003) Virtual Corporate Universities: A Matrix of Knowledge and Learning for the New Digital Dawn. Kluwer. Norwell.

Bruner J S (1966) Toward a Theory of Instruction. Belknap Press. Cambridge.

Chesbrough H W (2003) The Era of Open Innovation. MIT Sloan Management Review 4(3):74–81.

Coase R H (1937) The Nature of the Firm. Economica 4(16):386–405.

Dewey J (1966) Democracy and education: An introduction to the philosophy of education. The Free Press. New York.

Digenti D (1999) Collaborative Learning: A Core Capability for Organizations in the New Economy. The Society for Organizational Learning Journal 1(2):45–57.

Dosi G, Freeman C, Nelson R, Silverberg G, and Soete L (1988) Technical Change and Economic Theory. Columbia University Press. London.

Dunning J (1997) Alliance Capitalism and Global Business. Routledge. New York.

Eisenhardt K M and Sull D N (2001) Strategy as Simple Rules. Harvard Business Review 2001:106–116.

Freeman C and Perez C (1988) Structural Crisis of Adjustment. Business Cycles and Investment Behavior. In: Dosi G, Freeman C, Nelson R, Silverberg G, and Soete L (Eds.) Technical Change and Economic Theory. Columbia University Press. London.

Garvin D A (1993) Building a Learning Organization. Harvard Business Review 71(4):78–92.

Ghoshal S and Bartlett C A (1999) The Individualized Corporation. Harper Collins. New York.

Gibbons M, Limoges C, Nowotny H, Schwartzman S, Scott P and Trow M (1994) The New Production of Knowledge: The Dynamics of Science and Research in Contemporary Societies. Sage. London.

Harris J (2001) The Learning Paradox: Gaining Success and Security in a World of Change. Capstone. Oxford, UK.

Hayashi S, Kurokawa T (2009) Japan's Critical Issues on IT Human Resource, Science & Technology Trends 30:23–40.

Hitt M A, Ireland R D and Hoskinsson R E (2001) Strategic Management: Competitiveneness and Globalization. Southwestern. Oklahoma City.

Hitt M A, Ireland R D, Camp S M and Sexton D L (2002) Strategic Entrepreneurship: Integrating Entrepreneurial and Strategic Management Perspectives. In: Hitt M A, Ireland D R, Camp S M and Sexton D L (eds.) Strategic Entrepreneruship: Creating a New Mindset. Blackwell. Boston.

Kolb D A (1984) Experiential Learning: Experience as the Source of Learning and Development. McBer and Company. Boston.

Leonard-Barton D (1992) The Factory as a Learning Laboratory. Sloan Management Review 34(1):23–38.

Lipsey R G (1998) Technology Policies in Neo-Classical and Structuralist-Evolutionary Models. STI Review 22:31–74.

Malone T W (2004) The Future of Work – How the New Order of Business Will Shape Your Organization, Your Management Style, and Your Life. Harvard Business School Press. Boston.

Marquardt M J (2002) Building the Learning Organization. Davies Black. Palo Alto, CA.

McKnight W, Vaaler P M, and Katz R L (2001) Creative Destruction. MIT Press. Boston.

Piaget J (1977) The Development of Thought. Equilibration of Cognitive Structures. Basil Blackwell. Oxford.

Popper K R (1963) Conjectures and Refutations: The Growth of Scientific Knowledge. Routledge and Kegan Paul. New York.

Romano A (2008) Costruire l'Università Post-Fordista. Cacucci. Bari.

Romano A, De Maggio M and Del Vecchio P (2009) The Emergence of a New Managerial Mindset. In: Romano A (ed.) Open Business Innovation Leadership. Palgrave. London, UK.

Secundo G, Margherita A, Elia G, and Passiante G (2009a) A Service Science Perspective to Develop Engineering Systems Professionals, ASEE Global Colloquium on Engineering Education. 12th–15th October, 2009. Budapest. Hungary.

Secundo G, Margherita A and Elia G (2009b) Networked Learning for Human Capital Development. In: A. Romano (Ed.) Open Business Innovation Leadership. Palgrave. London, UK.

Siemens G (2004) Connectivism: A Learning Theory for the Digital Age. International Journal of Instructional Technology & Distance Learning. 2(1) http://www.itdl.org/Journal/Jan_05/article01.htm. Accessed 11 Dec 2009.

Silberglitt R, Antón P S, Howell D R and Wong A (2006) The Global Technology Revolution 2020 – In Depth Analyses. RAND Corporation. Santa Monica.

Skinner B F (1953) Science and Human Behavior. Macmillan. New York.

Tapscott D (1996). The Digital Economy. McGraw-Hill. New York.

Tapscott D (2006). Winning with the Enterprise 2.0. New Paradigm Learning Corporation. Toronto, Canada.

Tapscott D and Williams A D (2006) Wikinomics. Portfolio. London, UK.

Teece D, Pisano G and Schuen A (1997) Dynamic Capabilities and Strategic Management. Strategic Management Journal 18:509–533.

Venkatraman S and Sarasvathy S D (2001) Strategy and entrepreneurship: Outlines of an untold story. In: Hitt M A, Freema E, Harrison J S (eds.) Handbook of Strategic Management. Blackwell. Oxford.

Vest C M (2006) Educating Engineers for 2020 and Beyond. In: The Bridge 36(2):38–44. National Academy of Engineering (NAE). Washington.

Vygotskii L S (1978) Mind in society: The Development of Higher Mental Processes. Harvard University Press. Cambridge.

Watson J B (1913) Psychology as a Behaviorist View. Psychological Review 20(2):158–177.

Chapter 2
i-Communities as Cooperative Learning Spaces: The Case of the "Knowledge Forum"

Antonella Poce

Abstract The model devised in the first chapter is here developed taking as main "driving light" the concept of *interactivity:* one of the keywords that have been highlighted as the ideas around which *design, implement, deliver and monitor a learning experience contextualized in the open learning incubator.*

This chapter is centered, in fact, on the peculiarities of on line learning communities and it deepens topics related to the rise and development of social networking and the consequent creation of cooperative learning spaces. The aim is that of presenting a clear picture of the nature, potentialities and effective strengths of online learning communities that could represent the solution for the requirements our changing society is demanding.

Moreover, according to the paradigm shift which characterizes the model of the learning incubator, this chapter aims at discussing the pedagogical foundations of on line learning communities, the new role of the involved actors, the change of strategy, the different approach to contents and to the use of technology, the updated conception of space and time characterizing the learning dynamics.

Referring to the six dimensions highlighted in Chap. 1, this chapter can be represented by the following radar.

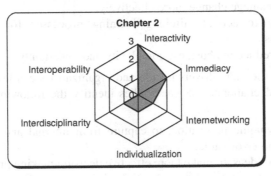

A. Poce (✉)
DIPED – Department for Educational Design, Università Roma TRE, Rome, Italy
e-mail: poce@uniroma3.it

Keywords i-Communities • Cooperative Learning Spaces • Knowledge Forum • Social Learning • Learning Community • Communities of practice • Learning Technologies

1 Cooperative Learning

In a rapidly changing environment, success of structured organizations depends on the ability to continuously self-reinvent for creating new sources of wealth and activating new opportunities of value creation.

In this scenario, learning processes play a strategic role because they are strictly linked to knowledge production and knowledge creation, two fundamental ingredients of the innovation cycle.

Learning processes are living a profound transformation in their strategic and operational approach, due to two interwoven factors: (a) the pervasiveness of the usage of the ICT, and (b) the diffusion of collaborative approach in competency development and knowledge application.

These two elements are at the basis of the topic discussed in this chapter, that is the importance of on line learning communities conceived as a new locus of competency development strategies. They enable the exploration of new knowledge domains and cooperative definition of new ideas and projects.

These communities act as distributed and networked environments, inspired to self-organization, co-evolution and fitness principles.

Actually, they represent a systemic answer to the following emerging challenges:

- intensification of the competition at global scale;
- new ways of organizing the work, mainly based on collaborative frameworks and mindset;
- the shortening of time spent for problem solving;
- the need to manage change more effectively;
- the urgency to activate lifelong learning processes for individuals and organizations;
- the need to reduce the business complexity and uncertainty.

But, which are the main drivers people and organizations can leverage on to face the above listed challenges? Some studies identify the following ones (Romano et al. 2009):

- open and dynamic innovation, to capture from internal and external sources potential sources of value;
- democracy of ideas, to make more effective decision making processes based on collective intelligence and active participation;
- creativity, to transform normal employee into extraordinary innovators;
- distributed leadership, to promote employees' responsibility and empowerment, and to diffuse leadership skills and behaviors at each organizational levels;
- lifelong learning, to make self-sustainable the competency update process, at individual and organizational level;

– new measurement systems, to capture and valorize both physical capital and intellectual resources.

These represent the main ingredients of cooperative learning approach, that wants to highlight not only the simple collaboration aspects based on exchange of codified knowledge and information, but primarily the way of working together, as peers of a dynamic community engaged in reaching common objectives, creating new knowledge, envisioning new ideas. This implies sharing of background knowledge, mixing of heterogeneous disciplines, reciprocal transferring of experiences, mutual enrichment, thinking and working with others.

In this perspective, this chapter explores the concept of interactivity, through presenting the main theoretical pillars and the applicative case of the Knowledge Forum.

1.1 Why Cooperative Learning Should be More Effective than Individual Learning: A Social Learning Theory Perspective

In order to understand why certain collaborative virtual learning environments are effective or not, it is important to reflect upon the theories that brought to the creation and employment of such tools. The issue here is why cooperative learning should be more effective than individual learning. One of the main reasons could be traced back in the so called *social learning theory* developed by Bandura in 1977. In particular, starting from behavioral studies, he realized that traditional behavioral conceptions of learning were not sufficiently accurate because did not take into consideration social influences. He distinguished between the acquisition of knowledge and the observable performance based on that knowledge (behavior). The idea was very simple and based on the consideration that everyone of us may know more than what we actually show.

Bandura realized in fact that cognitive factors such as beliefs, self perceptions and expectations influence learning. Accordingly, *social cognitive theory* distinguishes between *enactive* and *vicarious learning* (Woolfolk et al. 2008).

Enactive learning essentially is learning by doing and experiencing the consequences of one's actions. It is important to notice, in this respect, that this is not seen as *operant conditioning* but refers to a different role of consequences. *Operant conditioning*, in fact, has to do with strengthening or weakening of effect. In *enactive learning*, instead, consequences are seen as "providing information". Our interpretations of the consequences, therefore, favor expectations, build motivation and shape beliefs.

Vicarious learning allows learning by observing others. If we learn by observing other people in action, we engage cognitive factors, because we need to pay attention, construct images, remember, analyze, synthesize and so on and so forth. All the above processes imply an important mental activity, far from behaviorist conception according to which cognitive factors are unnecessary in the explanation of learning.

As Woolfolk and his colleagues underline (Woolfolk et al. 2008):

In social cognitive theory both internal and external factors are important: environmental events, personal factors (beliefs, expectations, and attitudes), physical and social environment (resources, consequences of actions, other people, and physical settings) and behavior (individual actions, choices and verbal elements). [...]. However, these behaviors also reciprocally impact upon personal factors. As learners achieve, their confidence and interest increase, for example, and behaviors also affect the social environment. If learners do not persist or if they seem to misunderstand, teachers may change instructional strategies of feedback. So the process of reciprocal determinism is dynamic and ongoing.

In *social cognitive theory*, *self-efficacy* and *self regulated learning* are key elements. *Self efficacy* is the ability to believe in our own capabilities of reaching a given objective (Bandura 1997). The list of sources of self efficacy expectations includes *vicarious experiences* and *social persuasion*. Both the above sources are present when collaborative environments are developed and established. In *vicarious experiences* the subjects involved in the group often see the others' accomplishments as models and when the model performs well, the learner's efficacy is enhanced, while it is decreased when it performs badly. As regards *social persuasion*, elements in the group can benefit from the others supporting and strengthening their potentials.

Increase of *self efficacy* is directly connected to motivation and to the setting of higher-level goals for students. This allows us to think that it should be prompted especially in virtual environments where lack of motivation and engagement is one of the main reasons for drop out. The advantage in online cooperative learning environments is the possibility of sharing and exchanging knowledge, creating new concepts and ideas, supporting each other and, therefore, fulfilling precise aims. It seems clear, however, that in such environments the continuous possibility to interact with the other subjects involved in the action of learning allows a sort of natural path to self-efficacy and therefore to the enhancement of a substantial change of attitude of all the subjects involved in the process.

1.2   Interactivity and Peer Working for Cooperative Learning

If we look at the history of pedagogy we realize that ideas related to learning can be found in the work of authors such as John Dewey's (Woolfolk et al. 2008): *In the early 1900s, John Dewey criticized the use of competition in education and encouraged educators to structure schools as democratic learning communities.*

It goes without saying, and it will be widely described in the next paragraphs, that today cooperative learning is strongly favored by the use of the Internet and the rise of web based communities. Participation in the web allows group discussion

Table 2.1 Cooperative learning forms (adapted from Woolfolk et al. 2008)

	Piagetian	Vygotskian
Group size	Small	Dyads
Group composition	Homogeneous	Heterogeneous
Tasks	Exploratory	Skills
Teacher role	Facilitator	Model/guide
Potential problems	Inactive/no conflict	Poor help giving
		Providing adequate time
Averting problems	Structuring controversy	Direct instruction in help giving
		Modeling help giving

and thus exchange of views and knowledge on particular topics of interest of the community itself. Interaction enhances continuous reorganization of knowledge, making frequent connections and revisions. The reason for success of social networking is to be found in the potentialities of interaction that the Web offers and advances in technology show that the above interactive relationships are every day closer and closer to face-to-face exchanges.

Table 2.1 describes the main characteristics of different forms of cooperative learning according to their theoretical origin (Woolfolk et al. 2008):

From the table above, different considerations can be argued: first of all that cooperative learning is not linked to the rise of the Internet but its advantages have been already identified when technological devices, normally in use today, were not even thinkable and, secondly, that, if purposes are clearly defined, cooperative learning can be designed accordingly.

Another aspect to be considered is that problem solving and project work are sort of tasks which fits within cooperative learning environment and the description, later on in this chapter, of technological devices built on purpose in this view, will show practical employment of such theories.

2 On Line Networks and Learning Community

In the article entitled *Building Technology–supported Learning Communities on the Internet*, that is part of the book *Learning to solve Problems with technology*, Margaret Riel, senior researcher at the SRI International – Centre for Technology in Learning at California State University, tells a story which is useful to understand the functions of a learning community (Jonassen et al. 2003).

Trying to involve her 4-year-old daughter in her work, she explains her how a modem works:

> *"You see these words on the screen. Well this little modem takes those words and turns them into sounds. They go on the telephone lines just like someone talking, and a computer on the other end is going to get them. Then that computer will send them to other computers. So my message will be sent all over the world."*
>
> *The child looked up from her colouring and said, "Oh like a talking drum" The mother, dumbfounded, finally asked, "A talking drum? You know a talking drum"? The mother thought some more, and then she remembered that not long ago, an African story teller had visited her daughter's preschool and shown the class an African drum. When villagers wanted to get a message out to neighbours about a festival or a market, they would use the drum, and the message would be sent from village to village.*

Man is a sociable animal and has always used his capabilities to communicate in order to reach his goals and survive. This makes it difficult, however, to understand why these abilities have not been adequately valued in traditional education.

Jonassen, director of the Study Centre for Problem Solving at the Missouri State University and expert in technology for education, reminds us again that Dewey himself dealt with the subject analysing the dangers that such a complex society as ours highlight:

"As societies become more complex in structure and resources, the need for formal teaching and learning increases. As formal teaching and training grows, there's a danger of creating an undesirable split between the experience gained in direct association and what is acquired in school."

(Dewey 1916)

If, as it seems a problem of continuity exists between what we learn from our experience of the world and formal education, a possible solution is offered by new technology which can, for instance, facilitate the work of learning communities.

There is an ever growing need for education and we do not often find consistency between what we learn from direct experience and institutional sources of education.

This reveals a sort of dual nature of learning: the one focused on traditional and formal learning activities, fixed place and well structured curricula; and the one characterized by informal style, unstructured programs, high-interactive relationships, peer evaluation, intensive usage of technologies and strong collaboration.

This last way finds its natural and effective organization within communities, a sort of network-based organization where people can interact and meet, where they have the possibility to enlarge the existing network, or to create new ones. The usage of technologies (internet, web, social networking, collaborative working environment, etc.) enables and accelerates the creation, the nurturing and the development of these learning networks, that could be conceived as formal or informal learning communities that have been set up for the primary purpose of enabling any kind of learning to take place over time for building capabilities, managing change, gain competitive advantage in the perspective of learning organization (Romano and Secundo 2009).

These new organizational forms, that can be recognized within a single organization or across different organizations, can be interpreted as particular forms of *"Communities of Practice"*, a concept proposed by J. Lave and E. Wenger in 1991 in their book entitled "Situated Learning: Legitimate Peripheral Participation" (Lave and Wenger 1991). In 1998, the same concept was further developed by E. Wenger in the book entitled "Community of Practice: Learning, Meaning and Identity" (Wenger 1998). Finally, in 2000, E. Wenger and W. Snyder published on the Harvard Business Review a specific article on this issue proposing the following definition:

"In brief, Communities of Practice are groups of people informally bound together by shared expertise and passion for a joint enterprise ...People in Communities of Practice share their experiences and knowledge n free-flowing, creative ways that foster new approaches to problems..."

(Wenger and Snyder 2000)

2.1 Communities of Practice

How to define a community of practice? First of all, it is important to say that not every community is a community of practice.

The term must be interpreted as a whole, focusing on the main features of an entity which is essentially characterised by a common way of acting. According to

Wenger, the essential conditions characterizing a community of practice are three (Wenger 1998):

- to share mutual engagement;
- to be engaged in a joint enterprise;
- to have a shared repertoire of facts and actions.

With regard to mutual engagement and, therefore, to the realisation of a "practice", Wenger considers that, this happens when people are engaged in actions whose meaning is the result of a process of negotiation with others.

Being part of a community is therefore the result of a common aim. Sharing an aim, being mutually engaged, however, does not imply necessarily the constitution of a group, of a net, of a team.

Belonging to a community is not linked to a specific social class and it is not defined by social interactions or geographical location.

Involvement within the community of practice is aroused by a series of reasons and frequently they are not so open. Sharing an aim is an important element but it is not the only one. The atmosphere that animates the community is another key for success. Working to keep that atmosphere is vital to the "practice" of the community.

It cannot be forgotten that sharing a common aim does not generate automatically a community made of homogeneous subjects. Each member is different from the other. A shared engagement compels to relate one's own experiences with those of the other ones.

A community of practice, then, is not free from conflicts and clashes too can be productive. Disagreement, competitiveness, challenge are all forms of participation.

Being involved in a *joint enterprise* helps the community to be bound together for three main reasons:

- it is the result of a process of negotiation which reflects the complexity of a shared engagement;
- it represents the accomplishment of the shared aim;
- it allows the establishment of mutual responsibilities among participants.

When a subject is involved in a group which subscribed a starting engagement, aiming at reaching a precise objective, it is also likely for the members of the community to have developed what Wenger calls a *shared repertoire*, i.e. the third requirement to be a *community of practice*.

As time goes by, in fact, actions performed to realise a *shared enterprise* produce resources to negotiate meaning. The repertoire, analysed here, can be made of a certain language, of the way of acting, making stories, gestures, symbols, concepts etc. that the community itself has produced from its start and that became part of its practice.

If the idea of *community of practice* developed by Wenger is clear, another definition given by Fulton and Riel let us go further. Even though they propose a synthesis of what has been explained above they complete the picture with a new element, the one that highlights how the actions performed with the community can facilitate knowledge building, as a result of the cooperative work of its members:

"A community of practice is a group of people who share a common interest in a topic or area, a particular way of talking about their phenomena, tools and sense-making approaches for self building their collaborative knowledge with a sense of common collective tasks."

(Fulton and Riel 1999)

Participating in a community of practice, then, allows learning naturally together with the others.

3   The Rise of the "i-Communities"

If the previous paragraph highlighted which are the learning dynamics that are carried out within environments where the subjects involved share a common aim, the present one attempts to explain how, in consideration of the above theories, *interactive* communities are created and how those changes of attitude, indicated in the paradigm shift, find their realisation in a different way of teaching and learning.

The origin of such shift, as far as the rise of technological learning communities is concerned, can be traced back to the research of Scardamalia and Bereiter carried out in the *C.S.I.L.E. (Computer Supported Intentional Learning Environments or Knowledge Forums)* project (Scardamalia 2004). They started from the consideration that school restrains knowledge building because it is centred only on the skills of the students. Past experience and acquired knowledge is not taken into consideration, unless it is not related to *curricula* topics. What students already know or think does not seem important (Jonassen 2004). Actually, it would be vital that also learning at school could be seen as an objective to reach in an active way and through adequate strategies. The authors conceived learning environments where students produce their archives of knowledge within learning communities. Doing so, knowledge can be represented openly to be evaluated, examined, and filled there where it presents gaps, revised and reworded (Scardamalia et al. 1994).

If students know a subject and use it, instead of referring only to the book or to the teacher, they feel immediately involved in the process of building and they do not remain passive just receiving information. Knowledge building becomes therefore a social activity (Jonassen et al. 2003) and it plays a fundamental role in community settlement, giving tools to store, organise and reformulate ideas which every member has proposed:

"Although these knowledge – building technology environments treat knowledge as a commodity, to the community of students it represents the synthesis of their thinking, something they own and for which they can be proud. In this sense, we believe, the goal of schools should be to foster knowledge – building communities."

(Jonassen et al. 2003)

A community is a social organisation made of people who share knowledge, values and objectives. Learning communities rise when students share the same interests and when they work together to reach a particular aim. Many of those communities facilitate reflection on background knowledge and on the processes adopted to build that knowledge.

With this regard, what Jonassen points out is essentially the fact that, instead of forcing students adapt themselves to traditional teaching methods, emphasis should be put on social and cognitive contribution that a group of learners gives to each of its components, thanks to their mutual cooperation, performed in the action of reaching a common objective (Jonassen et al. 2003). This way, it is possible to say that a *community of practice*, as Wenger conceived it, might be established and the main features of the shift from traditional to innovative teaching is carried out (Wenger 1998).

Online communication is different from face-to-face communication. It lacks important cues such as body language, voice, rhythm, accents, pace, pauses and other important aspects which contribute to define meaning.

Although this maybe limiting, it may also be helpful, as participants must take more care to see that they are communicating clearly. Online communication can happen also asynchronously and this even widens the range of opportunities, especially if we consider Gardner, who proposed the *Theory of Multiple Intelligences*, which suggests that intelligence is not a single capacity, but rather a series of distinct capabilities (Gardner and Lazear 1991; Gardner 2000). His studies suggest that rather than being smart to a certain degree, we should concentrate on how we are smart. People are often verbally deft and capable of carrying out stimulating conversations. They tend to do well in traditional school environments. Other people want more time to consider an idea and formulate their responses. When given a chance to think and then to speak, as it is in the case of several forms of online communication, these people experience a new freedom and level of participation. Everyone, therefore, can express him/herself according to his/her own abilities.

Table 2.2 shows how communication technologies facilitate a variety of learning activities, particularly those requiring collaboration and group effort (Jonassen et al. 2003).

It is important to underline that technology should be kept in support role and not become subject of the tool itself (Riel 1996):

"Building physical space should not be confused with building a community. A listserv, a conference, or a Web page, in and on itself, does not define a community… It is the interactions and partnerships among and between the people who gather in these places that define a community. […] These experiences do not replace face-to-place contacts anymore

Table 2.2 Online communication

Level	Learning activity
One-alone	Independent inquiry
	Research and writing browsing
One-to-one	Apprenticeship and internship
	Email and private consultations
	One on one chats
One-to-many	Lectures and symposiums
	Publishing results of research and enquiry activities
	Convenient access and dissemination of resources
Many-to-many	Debates, discussions
	Support of groups
	Group exercises and projects
	Interactive learning activities

than phone conversations replace meetings. They provide another form of social exchange that augment relationships and have real consequences."

The main issue is contained in the last line of the above quotation: the added value that technological tools can give teaching can be found in the peculiarities of the tools, which are more and more innovative, favouring interaction in a more and more realistic way. New tools, in fact, have the ability to rationalise and improve learning processes, allowing possibilities which support interpersonal exchange of knowledge and consequent building of new knowledge.

3.1 Technologies Enabling "i-Communities"

The environment which allowed the natural growth of learning communities is without any doubt the Internet which has acquired the dimension of a unique source to acquire precious information in every field of knowledge. The Internet is the means through which people and resources scattered all over the world can connect and interact. It is the only place where learners, teachers and every subject involved in a learning community can be linked and set free at the same time.

The constitution of a learning community can be stimulated by an assignment, or be self determined, for instance within listserv, chat lines or discussion groups. Communities, anyway, arise, as already pointed out, in places dominated by an atmosphere of trust, mutual support, sharing of the objectives and respect for diversity. Technology offers tools able to enlarge small communities that can rise in a limited environment, such as a school classroom, for instance, to include not only other classes but also other students, teachers, experts located in faraway places. Broadening the borders of the community, new information, projects and communication tools can enrich its value.

Technologies supporting learning communities offer the possibilities to understand the world and be open to the world more easily.

To this purpose, a possible mapping of learning technologies is shown in Fig. 2.1, where there is a classification based on two parameters: (a) the presence or not of a moderator, and (b) the typology of tools (synchronous or asynchronous).

Figure 2.1 highlights four classes of learning technological tools:

- Class 1: "Moderated and synchronous tools": they enable instantaneous communications involving different users that have to be on line. Moderators ensure an effective management of the communication. Examples of this category of tools are virtual classroom, audio–video conference systems, and chat rooms.
- Class 2: "Moderated and asynchronous tools": they enable communication among users, without any constraints of time and space. Actually, users can access on line at different time, by answering and interacting to pending messages and activities. A moderator ensures a coherence of the interventions and the animation of the community. Examples of this category of tools are assessment tools, forums, newsgroups, mailing lists, web learning systems.
- Class 3: "No moderated and synchronous tools": they ensure instantaneous communication, without any filtering process. Normally, they are used for on

	Synchronous Technologies	Asynchronous Technologies
Moderated technologies *(instructor, tutor, mentor)*	**1.** VC (Virtual Classroom) Audio-Video Conferencing Chat room	**2.** Assessments Forum Newsgroups Mailing List WBT (Web Based Training)
No moderated technologies (instructor, tutor, mentor)	**3.** Chat Room	**4.** Self Tests CBT (Computer based training) Forum Newsgroup Mailing list WBT (Web Based Training)

Fig. 2.1 Learning technologies

line coordination and exchange of messages. Examples of this category of tools are chat rooms, possibly integrated with Voice over IP systems.

- Class 4: *"No moderated and asynchronous tools"*: they ensure both empowerment of users and their individual and collective responsibilities. Besides, they offer major possibilities to reflection, analysis and deepening, typical of asynchronous environments. Examples of this category of tools are self-assessment tests, forums, newsgroups, mailing lists, computer training systems and web learning platforms.

Besides these tools, a set of social networking systems is arising and it proves to be a powerful instrument to start more effective learning processes. Examples of this category are blogs, wikis, podcasting services, RSS notifications, folksnomies. They enrich the user experience and they contribute to strengthen the relationships among community's members.

It is worth reminding that the *Cognition and Technology Group at Vanderbilt*, already in 1994, conceived a table of the values and principles animating learning communities, the so called *Peabody Perspective*, which contributes to highlight the pedagogical basis of a community of learners, as described in Table 2.3 (Jonassen et al. 2003).

As one can see from the table above the *Peabody Perspective* presents the strengths of the *Communities of Learners* according to five major areas of interest: curriculum, assessment, professional development, connection with the outer world and use of technology.

Some elements, among those highlighted, seem particularly meaningful and not taken for granted. The possibility to connect the Community with the outer world implies involving not only those who are naturally interested in what is going on, but also subjects located in other places and contexts.

Opening represents, therefore, a possibility of growth and enrichment which cannot be neglected. The role of technology becomes important then and must be taken into higher consideration allowing interaction at a distance and enlarging potentialities of the group engaged in the learning process.

Table 2.3 Peabody perspective

Curriculum	Assessment	Community connections	Professional development	Technology
Emphasis on active learning	Focused on communication	Shared responsibility	Learn and improve opportunities	Support all the areas of learning community
Problem focused learning	Authentic	Concern for common good	Professionals = facilitators	
Focus on project based activities				

We dealt with the possibility for learning communities to look for their members also outside their environment. Community begins with interactions among members, but it can also be strengthened and defined by its outside encounters.

As it has been said the above outside encounters can be supported by technological solutions *ad hoc* created. We discussed the potentialities of the Net as well some solutions that the Internet allows. Those potentialities, then, can be translated into a series of teaching strategies that Judi Harris has developed in a list of activity structures for the group, demonstrating the variety of activities that telecommunications enables: *interpersonal exchanges*; *information collection and analyses*; *problem solving projects* (Harris 2000).

In order to develop all the activities listed above, students must show some technological basic skills and they must meaningfully participate in conversations. In order to do that, they must be able to interpret messages, consider appropriate responses and construct coherent replies.

However, not all subjects can engage in coherent discourse. This is mainly due to the fact that students lack of practice in giving their own opinions about topics. They have always worked memorizing what other people tell them. It may be necessary to support people's attempts to converse.

It is interesting to notice that different points of contact can be identified, comparing the contents of the paradigm shift that guides the present work and both the *Peabody Perspective* and Judi Harris analysis. In particular the focus on active learning, interaction, problem based learning, sharing of knowledge, and so on, is almost unaltered.

4   The Case of the "Knowledge Forum"

A number of on line cooperative environments have been designed to support competency development, and among them *Knowledge Forum* is discussed here.

Knowledge Forum is a cooperative learning environment, a second generation product evolving from what researchers learned from its predecessor *CSILE*

(Computer Supported Intentional Learning Environment) developed by Marlene Scardamalia and Carl Bereiter from the Ontario Institute for Studies in Education.

As already mentioned, their investigation started already in the late 1980s when their interest in active learning brought them to develop the concept of communication within the class environment. What they realised, in fact, was that the organisation of interaction, communication and cooperation could lead to more effective learning outcomes and, in particular, to situations where knowledge could be built together rather than passively acquired.

When the first prototypes of the CSILE were introduced in the late 1980s, the main innovation was that restructured flow of information [...], questions, ideas and criticism suggestions were contributed to a public space equally accessible to all instead of it all passing through the teacher or (as email) passing as messages between individual students (Scardamalia and Bereiter 2006).

This meant also that, thanks to an organised structure, all contributors could mark their postings in ad hoc shelves, labelled as "My theory", "I need to understand", "New Information" and so on. It can be easily understood that information that in a face-to-face situation normally get lost in such a virtual environment were not only kept, but served as a basis for the development and for what the authors call *"idea improvement"*. This process implies a series of specific commitments:

- to progress;
- to seek common understanding;
- to expand the base of accepted facts.

It is easily arguable that these sorts of implications are recognizable as the objectives of scientists working in their laboratories. We are not accustomed to such structures in school or university learning environments, even if we are living in a "knowledge creating civilisation" and *the fundamental task of education is to acculturate youth into this knowledge creating civilisation and help them find a place in it* (Scardamalia and Bereiter 2006).

The experimentation and research activity performed by Scardamalia and Bereiter with school and university students involved in *Knowledge Forum* environments demonstrate that a different and more problem oriented approach to learning is possible, as in the "driving questions" of a research project.

It is of course a social constructivist theory of knowledge the one behind *Knowledge Forum* environments where "idea improvement" is founded on the concept that there is no thread of inquiry that cannot be improved and enriched through the exchange of views, concepts and consequent experimentation.

Knowledge Forum is built on such conceptions and it allows continuous revision as the theory evolves and new problems and issues are raised by the community.

The authors describe it as: *a multimedia database designed as to maximize the ability of a community of users to create and improve both its content and organisation. Thus the database itself is an emergent, representing at different stages in its development the advancing knowledge of the community.*

Its relevance with the topic under investigation in this chapter goes without saying, especially when we look at its design that is based on the creation of *views*

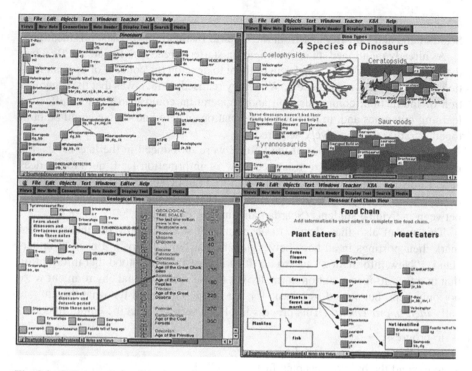

Fig. 2.2 Different views of the same notes on a Knowledge Forum environment

and *notes*. A view is *a sort of more articulated interpretation of the notes*. Different organisations of views and notes are always possible as Fig. 2.2 shows (Scardamalia and Bereiter 2006).

In the figure above, different views of the same notes are produced and it must be underlined that, in this particular instance, cooperative activities have been possible between school pupils and university students. These ones, in fact, being able to access the children "discourse", developed the subject of geological timeline that the children touched speaking of their favourite dinosaurs. When a biologist, then, has been asked to participate in the group, she contributed with the food chain view shown in the bottom right corner of the same picture.

It seems clear that continuous progressions of knowledge are possible and thanks to the contribution of very different subjects involved.

Notwithstanding the fact that *Knowledge Forum* has been tested and experimented mostly in schools and universities (in particular the Rose Avenue Public School in Toronto and the Institute of Child Study at the University of Toronto as well), it is used successfully, as the authors state (Scardamalia and Bereiter 2006), by *service and professional organisations, teacher development networks and businesses that are aiming to boost their imaginative capabilities.*

As it can be argued from the following paragraph, research conducted on *Knowledge Forum* showed its effectiveness and therefore aim of the authors is to develop it in more and more sophisticated updated editions.

Environments like the ones designed in *Knowledge Forum* allow the strengthening of a series of relevant aspects in teaching processes: learning abilities, problem solving skills, the change of the role played by the teacher within this sort of environments, and the possibility to assess students' products more efficiently.

As regards learning abilities, within *Knowledge Forum* contexts, students must get accustomed to critical thinking to negotiate meaning, they should learn to combine the different skills needed to write a good essay with those necessary to debate.

Face-to-face discussions tend to let the strongest personalities emerge, computers eliminates the differences and offer the same opportunities to everyone involved. Computers, then, help to classify information which are put at everyone's disposal.

If the group "works" in *problem solving*, discussions help decision making. If the problems faced are applicable to real situations, students will be facilitated when inserted in everyday contexts, once compelled to solve real problems.

In virtual environments like *Knowledge Forum*, teachers must coordinate discussions avoiding negligible discussions and so they operate as moderators who always drive attention to the main point. They are asked to avoid that anyone could make fun of anyone else's statements.

Continuously monitoring the situation, teachers have the opportunity to identify elements useful for assessment of students.

Learning assessment can be performed on the group as a whole or on the individual. Moreover, such a system allows to stop also on the processes adopted by the students to reach a result.

In summary, the key factors that characterise *Knowledge Forum*, as a valid example of interactive learning communities we can refer to, are strictly connected to the item of the paradigm shift mentioned in the previous paragraphs: the authenticity of the situations it proposes and the fact that the knowledge is directly produced by the students in *visible idea improvement*.

4.1 The Effectiveness of Knowledge Forum

A lot of research has been conducted by the authors of Knowledge Forum in order to prove the effectiveness of the tool they had created. It is sufficient to visit Knowledge Forum web site (www.knowledgeforum.com) to see some meaningful results.

A comparative study regarding the outcomes of the students engaged in knowledge building activities and those of a control group made of students, where no CSILE support was given, show that knowledge building students scored higher both on "basic skills" and "higher-level thinking".

More information about the control group are given on the website and stress meaningfulness of the results: *the Control class used in the research cited above was a class at a traditional school that does some group projects (without CSILE) as well as teacher-centered instruction. The other two groups include student communities who were on their first year of CSILE use or had already had a complete year of CSILE. Students were given the Canadian Test of Basic Skills (CTBS) at the beginning and the end of the school year. Improvement was measured by the post-test score, which was adjusted for group differences at pre-test by using an analysis of covariance.*

A study carried out in 1990–1991 describes how students in knowledge building classrooms performed better in language, reading, and vocabulary skills. Figure 2.3 below shows that improvement in "basic skills" for both first-year knowledge building students and second year knowledge building students.

Research also shows that knowledge building students could improve in higher-level thinking and learning skills. Results from Fig. 2.4 below show that students made greater progress over the course of the year in their ability to understand and use science concepts learned from difficult texts. The fact that the students working mainly on problem solving and recall abilities showed greater improvement in their performance in the fall pre-test and spring post-test is a good point to reflect upon. If we think of the need at the basis of the present study, tools as Knowledge Forum help perfectly the objective of facilitating the particular type of learning twenty-first century requires. Through effective cooperative learning, in fact, students not only improve their results but they gain abilities to be immediately employed in their working life.

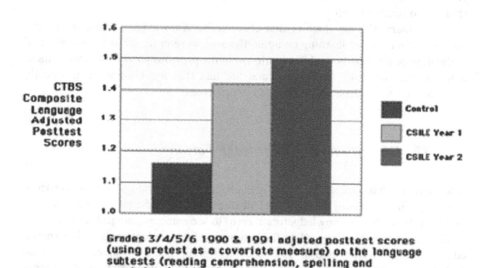

Grades 3/4/5/6 1990 & 1991 adjuted posttest scores (using pretest as a covariate measure) on the language subtests (reading comprehension, spelling and vocabulary) of the Conadian Test of Basic Skills.

Fig. 2.3 Test results with CSILE students – www.knowledgeforum.com

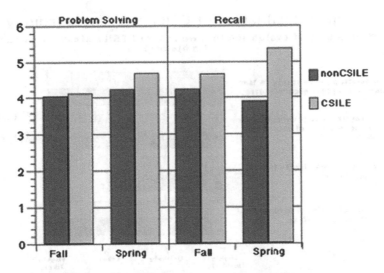

Fig. 2.4 Ratings on learning from difficult texts – www.knowledgeforum.com

As another measure of the effectiveness of knowledge building, experts and university-level students were asked to evaluate the quality of student work in the database. Not only was the quality of student comments found to be above standard in many cases, it also showed an increase in conceptual advancement. In addition, the quality of student research questions and the process of inquiry seemed to indicate to evaluators that there was a conscious effort on the part of students to clarify and explicate their research findings – a critical step in reaching new levels of understanding.

Another issue to be considered is that Knowledge Forum structure itself facilitates consistently students work toward conceptual enrichment. As the authors point out: *student research questions showed a high level of sophistication, and expert evaluation showed that the questions posed, if pursued, would likely lead to new conceptual understanding. The analysis of student research comments showed improvement in this sense.* Students engaged in knowledge building could demonstrate higher-order thinking, shifting from a functional and empirical frame of explaining physical phenomena towards a more theoretical frame of explanation. Self-organisation of study, moreover, marked a considerable advancement that is they succeeded in answering their research questions by finding explanatory scientific knowledge and by generating a series of more specific questions. It is worth with this regard quoting again the authors: *evaluators were particularly impressed with students' consistent and forceful way of requesting each other to clarify or explicate their work.* Researchers note that comments, which provide explanatory scientific information, are critical for advancement of students' inquiry. Particularly notable was *that student comments in the knowledge building environment provided analogies, which made new conceptual points of view available to the students who received them.*

Figure 2.5 presents some evidences of these observations.

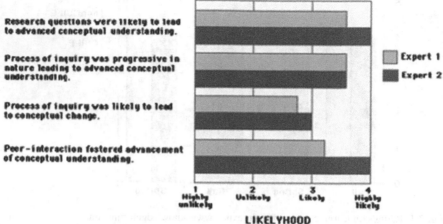

Fig. 2.5 Expert evaluation of CSILE student's inquiry – www.knowledgeforum.com

Another aspect highlighted by the authors of the research which is very consistent with the aims of the present study is represents by the demonstration that cooperative work is not necessarily related to lack of quality. This charge is usually attributed to a presumed lack of depth in analyzing materials or to the fact that only part of the group is actively working, while the others just make profit of the advancement of the group as a whole. Research, again, shows that low-level and high-level students interact with equal frequency on *Knowledge Forum* environments. The possibility to work anonymously help participation. Moreover, monitoring and coordinating each other's ideas increase in such environments.

Figure 2.6 below shows that cooperative skills gained and used in the knowledge building database were integrated in other situations. The authors observed that monitoring skills (such as awareness of and influence on peer ideas) showed a strong transference to face-to-face collaboration. In the test group using knowledge building software, students showed more monitoring of each other's ideas in face-to-face conversations, hence more useful collaboration overall.

Researchers pointed out also that the effectiveness of *Knowledge Forum* is related to the treatment of what they call misconceptions or mistaken thoughts, ideas, or notions. In traditional learning environments misconceptions can occur frequently and sometimes are difficult to be identified and corrected. In Knowledge Forum, misconceptions are either ignored or challenged. What researchers highlight is that students make considerable progress toward resolving misconceptions: in a knowledge building environment where students are not asked to prove what they know, but rather to explore their understanding, they can be surprisingly good at distinguishing what they really know from what they hypothesize or conjecture.

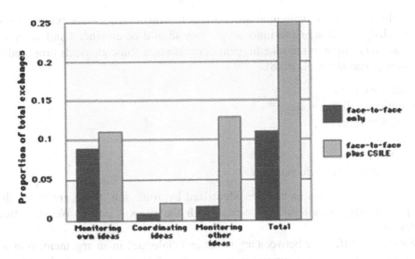

Fig. 2.6 Monitoring ideas during conversations – www.knowledgeforum.com

Frequency of Misconceptions

Number of notes in "force" unit	455
Instances of misconception or misinformation	122
Percentage of notes containing misconceptions or misinformation presented as information rather than as problem or conjecture	2%

How misconceptions were dealt with by CSILE students

Reinforced	3%
Ignored	60%
Partially resolved	27%
Resolved	10%

Fig. 2.7 Frequency of misconceptions – www.knowledgeforum.com

In the analysis of students' production, most misconceptions appeared in "problem", "theory", or "I need to understand" statements, just as misconceptions might arise in any university research hypotheses.

Figure 2.7 presents some evidences of these observations.

Again, as results shown above demonstrate, it is possible to state that cooperative learning carried out in ad hoc designed environments should be chosen as a new way of teaching and learning if we are really seeking the advancement of knowledge.

5   Discussion and Conclusions

In conclusion, if learning communities are to be considered successful facilitators of knowledge exchange and innovation, they should be enhanced and favoured. To do so, it is important to take in great consideration some elements proposed by Jonassen (Jonassen et al. 1998):

- communication;
- attention to differences;
- shared culture;
- adaptation;
- dialogue;
- access to information resources.

Among the various categories identified by Jonassen, there are some that are particularly meaningful in respect with the present paper. We start from *Dialogue*.

What's the difference between argument and dialogue? In an argument, your job is to define a position and support it, to the point of convincing your advocate or a third party of the superiority of your position. A true conversation or dialogue is something different. You actually listen to the personal across from you with the hope of learning something new. Dialogue, in the best sense, is not oppositional or confrontational; rather, it is just the opposite. Dialogue involves a willingness to suspend one's beliefs in favour of listening to another, to surrender and give up one's position if doing so serves the needs of the group.

What is underlined in the above quotation is the importance of letting the exchange of knowledge occur, through dialogue.

The second category is *attention to differences*.

Like all complex adaptive systems, learning communities thrive on differences. Every group member shares some things in common with the group and holds other things unique. Most differences among group members go no further than the individual learner; however, every so often a different perspective or strategy will be found to have utility within the group as a whole.

In this case, the main aspect to be taken into consideration is the fact that diversity represents the richness of the community and must be sought and enhanced.

In conclusion, if every aspect underlined by Jonassen is important to favour successful communities, the role of technology in support of the above objectives becomes fundamental and is the real key to the development of learning places in tune with the requirements of the society we live in.

Finding out strategic paths to let the creation of successful cooperative learning communities represents a considerable engagement for all the subjects involved, but this is an effort that is rewarded by the valuable results that learning carried out in social environments can tribute.

References

Bandura A (1997) Self-efficacy the Exercise of Control. Freeman. New York.

Dewey J (1916). Democracy and Education. An Introduction to the Philosophy of Education. 1966 Edition. Free Press. New York.

Fulton D and Riel M (1999) Collaborative Online Continuing Education: Professional Development Through Learning Communities. http://glef.org. Accessed 22 Jan 2010.

Gardner H (2000) Intelligence Reframed: Multiple Intelligences for the 21st Century. Basic Books. New York.

Gardner H and Lazear D (1991) Seven Ways of Knowing, Teaching for Multiple Intelligences: A Handbook of the Techniques for Expanding Intelligence. Hawker Bronlow Education. Victoria.

Harris J (2000) Structuring Internet-Enriched Learning Spaces for Understanding and Action. Learning and Leading with Technology, 28(4). www.iste.org. Accessed 10 Jun 2009.

Jonassen D H (2004) Handbook of Research on Educational Communications and Technology. Second Edition. Lawrence Erlbaum Associates. Mahwah.

Jonassen D H, Kyle C P and Brent G W (1998) Creating Technology – Supported Learning Communities. In: Jonassen D H, Kyle C P and Brent G W (eds.) Learning With Technology in the Classroom: A Constructivist Perspective. Merrill/Prentice-Hall. New York.

Jonassen D H, Howland J, Moore J and Marra R M (2003) Building Technology – Supported Learning Communities on the Internet. In Jonassen D H, Howland J, Moore J and Marra R M (ed.) Learning to Solve Problems With Technology. Merril Prentice Hall. Upper Saddle River.

Lave J and Wenger E (1991) Situated Learning: Legitimate Peripheral Participation. University of Cambridge Press. Cambridge.

Riel M (1996) The Internet: A Land To Settle Rather Than An Ocean To Surf And A New Place For School Reform Through Community Development. http://gsh.lightspan.com/teach/articles/netasplace Accessed 19 Nov 2009.

Romano A and Secundo G (2009). Dynamic Learning Networks. Models and Cases in Action. Springer. New York.

Romano A, De Maggio M, Del Vecchio P (2009). The Emergence of a New Managerial Mindset. In Romano A (ed.) Open Business Innovation Leadership – The Emergence of the Stakeholder University. Palgrave Macmillan. New York.

Scardamalia M (2004) CSILE/Knowledge Forum. In: Kovalchick A and Dawson K (eds.) Education and Technology: An Encyclopedia. ABC-CLIO. Santa Barbara.

Scardamalia M and Bereiter C (2006) Knowledge Building: Theory, Pedagogy and Technology. In: Sawyer K (ed.) Cambridge Handbook of the Learning Sciences. Cambridge University Press. New York.

Scardamalia M, Bereiter C and Lamon D (1994) The CSILE Project: Trying to Bring the Classroom into World 3. In: McGilly K (ed.) Classroom Lessons: Integrating Cognitive Theory and Classroom Practice. MIT Press. Cambridge.

Wenger E (1998) Communities of Practice: Learning, Meaning and Identity. CUP. New York.

Wenger E and Snyder W (2000) Community of practice: The organizational frontier. Harvard Business Review, Jan–Feb:139–145.

Woolfolk A, Hughes M and Walkup V (2008) Psychology in Education. Pearson Longman. Harlow.

Chapter 3
Problem-Based Learning in Web Environments: The Case of "Virtual eBMS" for Business Engineering Education

Gianluca Elia, Giustina Secundo, and Cesare Taurino

Abstract This chapter presents a case study where Problem Based Learning (PBL) approach is applied to a Web-based environment. It first describes the main features behind the PBL for creating Business Engineers able to face the grand technological challenges of the 2020. Then it introduces a Web Based system supporting the PBL strategy, called the "Virtual eBMS". This system has been designed and implemented at the e-Business Management Section of the Scuola Superiore ISUFI – University of Salento (Italy), in the framework of a research project carried out in collaboration with IBM. Besides the logical and technological description of Virtual eBMS, the chapter presents two applications of the platform in two different contexts: an academic context (international master) and an entrepreneurial context (awareness workshop with companies and entrepreneurs). The system is illustrated starting from the description of an operational framework for designing curricula PBL based from the author perspective and, then, illustrating a typical scenario of a learner accessing to the curricula. In the description, it is highlighted both the "structured" way and the "unstructured" way to create and follow an entire learning path.

Referring to the six dimensions highlighted in Chap. 1, this chapter can be represented by the following radar:

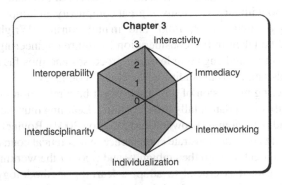

G. Elia (✉)
Euro-Mediterranean Incubator – Department of Engineering Innovation, University of Salento, Lecce, Italy
e-mail: gianluca.elia@unisalento.it

G. Elia and A. Poce (eds.), *Open Networked "i-Learning": Models and Cases of "Next-Gen" Learning*, DOI 10.1007/978-1-4419-6854-8_3,
© Springer Science+Business Media, LLC 2010

Keywords Problem-based learning • Virtual eBMS • Business Engineering Education • "Right" learning • Personalized learning

1 Introduction

Nowadays engineering disciplines and professionals are more and more important drivers of economic progress and quality of life for the society. In the coming decade, engineers will face big challenges such as make solar energy economical, improve urban infrastructure, prevent nuclear terror, develop carbon sequestration methods, enhance health informatics, secure cyberspace, engineer the tools of scientific discovery, re-engineer the brain, enhance virtual reality, manage the nitrogen cycle, and advanced personalized learning (NAE 2004). Some radical revolutions have increased the importance of these complex and integrated systems in today's world.

First, after the last century's major discoveries such as electrification, airplane, radio and television, computers, nuclear technologies, and high-performance materials (NAE 2005), a real revolution is today brought by breakthrough innovations like "bio", "nano", "cogno" and "information" technologies. Second, breakthrough technology innovations determine non-linear phenomena and processes which require non-linear thinking and mindset. Third, a number of other forces change the world in the twenty-first-century, such as globalization, radical transformation of the workforce and workplace, increased customer influence, and emergence of learning as major organizational asset (Marquardt 2002). Historically, changes in the engineering education have followed changes in technology and society with the purpose to meet the critical issues and provide the workforce required to integrate new developments into the economy. However, the intensity and speed of changes today make this endeavor more difficult.

The engineer of tomorrow will have to face two major sets of challenges related to scale and increasing complexity (Secundo et al. 2009b). The first has to do with smaller spatial scales and faster time scales, the world of bio/nano/info whereas the second has to do with larger systems of great complexity and importance to society, such as energy, environment, food, and manufacturing (Wright 1999). These aspects should be taken in full consideration by future engineering education, also to build more active and engaging learning processes and thus face the decrease of interest towards engineering studies in developed countries.

The engineering profession of tomorrow won't be a reflection of the engineering of today but rather a fundamentally different thing. Learning must be affective as well as cognitive and behavioural (Brownell and Jameson 2004). Bovinet (2000) observed that while students may demonstrate competence in theoretical courses, they are often ineffective when dealing with the ambiguity and rigor of the working world.

In this scenario, it is crucial to adopt a learning methodology that is mainly based on problems definition and solving, with which the learner can autonomously acquire the necessary amount of knowledge, following both structured curricula and mainly unstructured programs, to face and solve specific problems and, as a consequence, can improve his/her competences and skills. In order words, a *Problem Based Learning (PBL)* approach is required (Ward and Lee 2002).

This chapter presents two case studies: the first one is focused on the application of the PBL approach in Web-based environments for creating the Engineers of the future, within an International Master. The second case study concerns two awareness workshops with companies and entrepreneurs of tourism and agro-industry. Both cases have been designed and implemented by the e-Business Management Section (eBMS) of the Scuola Superiore ISUFI – University of Salento (Italy).

The rest of the chapter is organized as follows: The Sect. 2 describes the main theory background underpinning the choice of PBL approach for Engineering Education; the Sect. 3 illustrates the process through which engineers acquire competence through PBL; whereas the Sect. 4 describes the two case studies respectively in academic and entrepreneurial contexts. The Sect. 4 includes also a comprehensive description the Virtual eBMS concerning the logical and technological architectures, as well as the set of services and the description of learning scenarios. Finally, some discussions and conclusions are reported in Sect. 5.

2 Why PBL Approach for Engineering Education?

If the hallmark of engineering education in the twentieth-century was a science revolution which led to learning patterns designed to teach engineers through science-based courses, the ongoing fusion of science with technology (called *"scitech revolution"*) will affect the engineering disciplines in the twenty first century, blurring the distinction between engineering and science (Tadmor 2006). Engineers of tomorrow must be able to conceive and manage projects of enormous complexity that require a highly integrative view of engineering systems (Vest 2006). Within the context of professional engineering practice, the efforts to look at complex interconnected systems should include: (a) the application of engineering processes to define and solve complex engineering problems; (b) the engagement of the engineer from different disciplines in team-based problem-solving processes; (c) the interaction of the engineer with the customer and managers to set shared goals; (d) the economic, political, ethical, and social constraints as boundary conditions (NAE 2005).

In analogy with a product's life cycle, also the knowledge and experience that are at the foundations of competencies have a life cycle and can thus become obsolete. Thus, when a competence is declining, the need to develop a new competence or enhance/update the old one arises (Secundo et al. 2009a).

The challenge today is not simply training engineers to acquire specialized competencies and knowledge but rather developing self learning attitudes to make sustainable the lifelong learning processes, as well as to rethinking education systems to address complex problems in the logic of engineering systems. In particular, there is a need to ensure that the core knowledge advances in information technology, nano-science, biotechnology, materials science, photonics, and other areas yet to be discovered are delivered to engineering students so they can leverage them to achieve interdisciplinary solutions to engineering problems (NAE 2005).

The new engineering education must take into account that in the future students will learn in a completely different way and they should be focused on solving unknown problems (Vest 2006). Innovation in engineering education will be addressed on designing innovative learning environments (ASEE 2009), where learning patterns contents should be designed around the "grand technological challenges" (NAS 2008). Actually, the real challenge is to design learning environments based on the web, focused on systemic and interdisciplinary curricula with strong emphasis on design, creativity, innovation and entrepreneurship.

These environments can be conceived as a learning laboratory (Leonard-Barton 1992), i.e. "a constructed microcosm of real-life settings where teams can learn how to learn together, combining meaningful business issues with meaningful interpersonal dynamics" (Senge 1990). The laboratory can enhance systematic problem solving and discovery, experimentation of new approaches, learning from past histories, learning from external experiences and best practices, transferring knowledge quickly and effectively (Garvin 1993). The learning laboratory stimulates three kinds of learning processes: "experiential knowledge" learning processes, "emerging knowledge" learning processes, and "formalized knowledge" learning processes. Specifically, formalized knowledge refers to well defined and consolidated concepts and theories, a sort of "compass" to explore new contexts and problems. Experiential knowledge refers to new insights and concepts experimented during context-based applications, and that confirm existing theories and approaches. Emerging knowledge refers to new ideas and hypothesis extracted from context-based experiences, and that open new conceptual spaces for rethinking theoretical frameworks, models and strategies (Elia et al. 2001).

Concerning the learning strategy, field literature has highlighted the evolution from the idea of learning as transferring knowledge and shaping people to a new concept of learning as "travelling" and "growing". The metaphor of travel refers to the idea that a teacher guides the students through an unknown terrain that needs to be explored. The teaching methods are thus experiential such as simulations, projects, problems, exercises with unpredictable outcomes, research projects, discussions, brainstorming and independent learning. The growing metaphor is an extension of the travelling more focused on the idea of self-initiative of the student whose aim is to develop his/her own personality (Baets 2003).

These metaphors require a fundamental rethinking of learning methods, from course-based, one-to-many, and off-line provisioning, to application-based, peer-to-peer, and on-line interactions (Romano et al. 2005).

With this new approach learners and engineers should be allowed to learn at their own rhythm or in a self-paced way and becoming responsible for their learning process, which happens "in action", rather than in "classroom". This entails a substantial shift from traditional, course-based learning approaches to context-aware, just-in-time, individualized learning strategies and processes (Secundo and Passiante 2007) in which the problem becomes the overall context of the learning processes.

PBL holds great promise for using a prototypical, real-world problem as the focus for student-centered active learning. With this approach, students are better able to develop competencies in the often neglected affective learning dimension (Brownell and Jameson 2004).

3 How do Engineers Acquire Competence Through PBL?

By now, it is widely recognized and accepted that the activation of effective processes represents one of the main challenges for every industry and organization (Stojanovic et al. 2001). The incredible velocity and volatility of today's markets require just-in-time methods for supporting the need-to-know, as well as the readiness and the immediacy to act of employees. Thus, the new style of learning will be driven by the requirements of the new economy: efficiency, immediacy, just-in-time delivery and task relevance (Stojanovic et al. 2001).

Therefore, learning processes need to be fast and just-in-time. Speed requires not only a suitable content of the learning material (highly specified, not too general), but also a powerful mechanism for organizing such material (Stojanovic et al. 2001). Moreover, learning must be a customized on-line service, initiated by user profiles and business demands. In addition, it must be integrated into day-to-day work patterns and needs to represent a clear competitive edge for the business (Adelsberger et al. 2001).

As a consequence, learners and knowledge workers have to generate specific learning processes that should be increasingly fast and effective. On the other way, "right" (effective) learning strategies have to guarantee (Schmidt and Winterhalter 2004):

- delivered knowledge must be relevant to the knowledge workers' activities and properly structured and described for solving their problems and/or perform their tasks *(right knowledge)*;
- delivered knowledge must be modeled around the knowledge workers' profile *(right way)*;
- delivered knowledge must be delivered according to the knowledge workers' learning style *(right people)*;
- learning process must be triggered just-in-time *(right time)*.

Therefore, traditional processes for content development and delivery, characterized by a lack of dynamism and flexibility in creating and structuring content, as well as by a rigid and predefined timing for the delivery phase, are no more efficient and adequate. A radical change is needed both in designing the content architecture and in the strategy for content delivery. So, it reveals necessary to radically innovate:

- models for the content architecture, by promoting an *interdisciplinary approach* for structuring the learning content;
- ways for accessing to the learning content, by delivering based both on *just-in-time* and *unstructured* learning.

Being inspired to these principles, Problem Based Learning (PBL) approach incorporates naturally an interdisciplinary vision of the knowledge architectures.

This is possible because a problem's solution requires the synergic contribution of more disciplines. Besides, PBL approach ensures an "on line" and interactive relationships and experiences that are not based on a fixed and scheduled path, but they are grounded on a research activity of possible alternatives, on their evaluation, on their application, on a real-time management of their feedbacks to improve and enhance the final solution.

PBL approach situates learning in a meaningful task, such as case-based instruction and project-based learning. In the traditions of Kilpatrick and Dewey, this approach argues for the importance of practical experience in learning (Kilpatrick 1918, 1921; Dewey 1938).

In PBL, students learn by solving problems and reflecting on their experiences (Barrows and Tamblyn 1980). PBL is well suited to helping students become active learners because it situates learning in real-world problems and makes students responsible for their learning (Hmelo-Silver 2004). It has a dual emphasis on helping learners develop strategies and construct knowledge (Collins et al. 1989; Hmelo and Ferrari 1997; Kolodner et al. 1996). PBL has two distinct goals:

- to learn a required set of competencies or objectives;
- to develop problem-solving skills that are necessary for lifelong learning (Engel 1991).

According to PBL, a problem (not flat lessons, exercises, or other structured material) is assigned to the learner, and the learner has to autonomously search all the information he needs to solve that problem. In this way the learner has a proactive role in his own learning experience and becomes responsible for his competences growth.

After an examination of recent implementations, the main features of the PBL strategy are (Ward and Lee 2002) (Engel 1991):

- unstructured problems, that simulate real life situations often characterized by ambiguity and complexity, in which they do not have one single correct answer; they promote inquiry-based behaviors, they stimulate curiosity and open mind approach in formulating a solution;
- an interdisciplinary approach, that guarantee a complete analysis of the problem statement in order to propose an effective a complete solution;
- teacher as mentor and learning facilitator, involved in selecting the problem, present it to the learners and then providing them direction for research and inquiry, keeping them highly involved in the overall learning process;
- action oriented and experiential learning, that promote active participation of learners and effective consolidation and update of mental schemas.

A critical element in this change is the recognition of the need to redesign and integrate the traditional business curricula (Vesper 1973) and to create new knowledge architectures supporting problem solving approach and inquiring learning.

In the next paragraph a case study illustrating the development of the Business Engineer competencies using a Problem Based Learning approach in a Web Environment will allow explaining how these concepts are implemented in practices.

4   Creating Business Engineers Using a PBL Approach in Web Environment: Two On-field Applications

With the progressive diffusion of Information and Communication Technology (ICT), Web Based Learning Environments provide both collaborative and self-paced learning services with empowered functionalities that conventional face-to-face classroom couldn't provide.

Starting from this consideration, and taking into account the importance of the PBL methodology for creating business engineers in the emerging competitive environment, here we would like to illustrate how to design and implement PBL curricula in Web Based Environment for creating the Business Engineer profile.

We will proceed by describing a case study in action aimed to develop the Business Engineer competencies using a Problem Based Learning approach in a Web Environment at the e-Business Management Section (eBMS) of the Scuola Superiore ISUFI – University of Salento (Italy). The case is described starting from the description of the operational framework for designing PBL based curricula and, then, illustrating a typical scenario of a learner who accesses to an on line curricula focused on the "Extended Enterprise" domain. The case illustrates also the web based environment, named "Virtual eBMS", conceived to facilitate and practice the PBL methodology within the above mentioned curricula.

4.1   The Business Engineer Profile

As for "Business Engineer" we mean an archetype of modern engineer who is able to identify and exploit the potential of ICT for reconfiguring traditional business processes and organizational models. This profile is grounded on interdisciplinary knowledge building blocks such as internet-worked business, global management, technological entrepreneurship, organizational learning, innovation and leadership, strategic management, internet business management and e-business design and implementation (Secundo et al. 2009a).

The "Business Engineer" profile can be considered as a real archetype of adaptive innovator (University of Cambridge and IBM 2008), i.e. a person who possesses highly specialized competencies in one discipline but also broad knowledge and system thinking ("T-shaped"). He/she is able to work in the perspective of open collaboration and collective intelligence to solve complex issues.

In fact, the "business engineer" is a person able to integrate strategic, organizational and digital innovation to develop new business models and accelerate business transformations. He/she should act as specialist, integrator and change agent at the same time. He/she has to be a *specialist*, providing expertise of world-class standing; he/she is an *integrator* since works in multicultural teams and global environments, managing across boundaries and combining technical, organizational and managerial capabilities in a complex environment, and operates with flexibility and according to high ethical standards. Finally, he/she is a *change agent* since adapts to a changing business environment, recognizes opportunities and manages change, reconfigures traditional business models towards the extended enterprise, uses creativity and entrepreneurial spirit in business and technology innovation, leads change and learns lifelong, shaping the uncertain future.

As "specialist", the business engineer requires "contextual competencies", i.e. job-related and role-specific competencies; whereas as "integrator" he/she needs "generic competencies", i.e. more abstract and transferable competencies applied across organization. Finally, as "change agent", he/she should possess changing competencies, i.e. competencies suitable to innovate in the transforming context.

Table 3.1 shows an illustrative list of the different types of competencies of a Business Engineer.

4.2 The Interdisciplinary Knowledge Base Supporting the "Extended Enterprise" Domain

Many of today's most complex and pressing challenges for engineering education require innovative and interdisciplinary approaches. Challenges such as making healthcare affordable and accessible, managing global manufacturing and supply chains, rebuilding crumbling infrastructures, and working toward energy security don't have purely technical solutions. To address these challenges, engineering students should be thus engaged in interdisciplinary learning patterns and projects that require them to put theory into practice, improving capacity for lifelong learning and enhancing management skills.

Table 3.1 Competencies of the business engineer

Contextual competencies (Engineer as "specialist")	Generic competencies (Engineer as "integrator")	Changing competencies (Engineer as "change agent")
Ability to conceive and design complex engineering systems	Ability to work effectively in and multicultural environments	Ability to adapt in a changing environment
Ability to frame complex problems	Business knowledge	Ability to apply theory to practice decision making
Analytical skills	Capacity to synthesize engineering, business and societal perspectives	Ability to recognize and manage the change
Engineering fundamentals	Communication skills	Constant curiosity
Project management	Dynamism and flexibility	Creativity
Technical leadership	High ethical standards	Entrepreneurial spirit
	Interpersonal skills	Leadership capabilities
	Strong professionalism	Persistent need to learn
	Team working	Social, global and political awareness

By definition, interdisciplinary teaching starts with a topic, theme, problem, or project that requires active student participation and knowledge of multiple disciplines in order to reach a resolution (Dabbagh et al. 2000; Gordon et al. 2001; Meier et al. 1996; Sage 2000; Tchudi and Lafer 1996). Rather than composing a disciplinary bundle, the first step for the faculty or responsible of a learning module is to define a core problem or challenge and then to identify which knowledge areas are relevant or may contribute to the solution of the problem. This approach has roots in Socratic inquiry and centuries-old apprenticeship training. Socrates did not lecture as much as he moderated and directed questioning. It can be observed in The Republic by Plato (360 B.C.E./1960) that Socrates guided his students through inquiry to answer their own questions, search out answers to problems, and relate their knowledge to life applications.

In the same logic, it is possible to refer to the study of the "extended enterprise" as "challenges-generating" domain that impacts at organizational level, at people management level, at policy/regulation level, at technology level, at management and strategic level (Secundo et al. 2009b).

Actually, once identified the problem or challenge, the learning responsible became the mentor that provides learners with some insights and fundamental issues related with the different areas. The deepening and search for further relevant knowledge is then left to the curiosity and creative exploration of the learner.

The solutions identified have two major results as they allow addressing the problem as well as contributing to further develop knowledge areas originally involved. In this sense, the system is open and self-developing as the nature and volume of knowledge "incubated" for learning purposes varies and evolves in a way which is non-linear and non-predefined.

4.3 "Virtual eBMS": A Web-Based System Supporting the PBL Approach

The "Virtual eBMS" platform has been designed and developed at the e-Business Management Section (eBMS) of the Scuola Superiore ISUFI, University of Salento (Italy), by integrating different market products and some components developed ad hoc (Secundo et al. 2008).

The "Virtual eBMS" is conceived as a Collaborative Working Environment enabling knowledge sharing, knowledge exchange and collaborative learning processes, in the perspective to support and enhance Intellectual Capital growth.

Before starting the design phase of the "Virtual eBMS", the project team conducted both a benchmarking of the existing web learning and knowledge management platforms available on the market, and a deep analysis of the educational and research activities and practices at eBMS, in order to gather the required information to set up a complete and efficient platform useful for the delivery of effective on line learning patterns. This analysis had a specific focus on PBL approach applied to the higher education programs.

4.3.1 The Logical Architecture and the Services Characterizing the "Virtual eBMS"

The "Virtual eBMS" system integrates natively Web Learning and Knowledge Management components to build a Global Learning Community, both from the organizational and the technological point of view, in which to define rich and effective learning experiences (Romano et al. 2001). The overall system is completely web-based, and it can be easily linked to other Web-based systems, so allowing a high level of flexibility and extensibility. In the implemented version, as shown in Fig. 3.1, there are some external links with:

- an *e-Business platform* to experiment the applications and business processes of an enterprise collaborating in network within industrial cluster. This platform has been specialised and customised in the domain of tourism, realising a DMS (Destination Management System) and in the domain of agri food, developing a Digital Marketplace;
- a *Multimedia Laboratory*, for the acquisition, production, storage and distribution, also in streaming, of multimedia contents.

For the original approach adopted to integrate web learning and knowledge management sub-systems, and for the innovativeness of the PBL methodology embedded within the system, in 2006 "Virtual eBMS" got the "2006 Brandon Hall Excellence in Learning Award", in the learning technology category.

The service categories of the "Virtual eBMS" are articulated into five main distinct functional components, as shown in Fig. 3.2:

- knowledge management service component;
- project management service component;
- web learning service component;
- collaboration service component;
- e-business service component.

These five components are complemented by the "cross-layer" service component.

Fig. 3.1 An integrated view of the "Virtual eBMS"

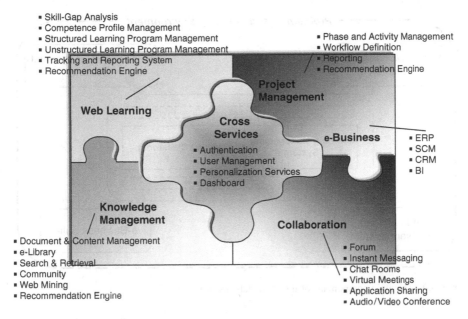

Fig. 3.2 The service categories of the "Virtual eBMS"

The following section deepens the Web Learning component, with a particular focus on the Problem Based Learning layer.

4.3.2   The Web Learning Component of the "Virtual eBMS"

Referring to the web learning component of "Virtual eBMS", we would like to highlight the most interesting characteristics of the system, which allows learners to enter into a new web-learning environment in which they can experiment a new pedagogical approach, with the final goal to make possible a more effective learning process.

The basic innovation for this system consists in the creation of a new web learning environment in which learners, mentors and tutors can interact all together for competence growth, for educational "coaching", and for facilitating the learners' activities, according to the problem-based learning strategy.

The environment was obtained by implementing an independent software layer that uses the public APIs of a traditional Learning Management System (LMS) integrated with a Virtual Classroom (VC) system. This represents the engine of the platform, opportunely connected with other "internal" small components useful to perform specific tasks, and collaborating with "external" and self-consistent platforms (a knowledge management system, a project management tool, an e-business suite, an audio-video streaming delivery system) to ensure a complete and effective learning experience.

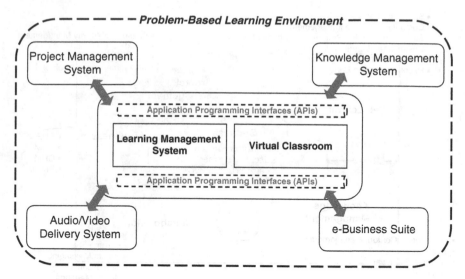

Fig. 3.3 The main components of the PBL web environment

All these platforms have a high level of interoperability obtained through a strong integration of data sources, knowledge bases and learning resources and activities/events (Elia et al. 2009).

Figure 3.3 shows the main components of the whole PBL Web Environment.

As for the main **processes** enabled by the platform, they are:

- *skill-gap analysis and competence profile management*, to manage effectively several categories of profiles and to provide learners with a self self-assessment process;
- *structured learning program management*, to implement and deliver structured learning experiences, based on a formal enrollment and a pre-defined curriculum of on line courses;
- *unstructured learning program management*, to allow learners to self-define their own learning programs through a dynamic selection of contents, modules and resources useful to solve a problem or execute a task;
- *curricula monitoring/reporting and competence tracking*, to ensure a complete overview about the competence progresses and an efficient update of the learners' profile;
- *recommendation* to provide further resources, modules and "learning pills" based on personal interests and competence profile status.

As for the **contents** that feed the learning base, they are constituted by:

- *competence taxonomy*, considered as the backbone of the learning base, is organized with a three-level structure: (1) the application domain it refers to; (2) the specific competence in the domain, with three possible levels of expertise (aware, competent, expert); (3) the learning objective, that identify a specific task or ability;

- *competence profile*, represented by a set of competencies, with a specific level of expertise, and contextualized into a specific domain;
- *SCORM objects*, the traditional learning objects created according to the international standard SCORM, and usually associated to a specific learning objective;
- *multimedia knowledge objects*, aggregations of heterogeneous files, integrated by additional references to external links and physical resources, usually associated to a specific learning objective;
- *multimedia learning modules*, representing the basic item for creating a complete curriculum. It includes a set of multimedia resources, traditional courseware, individual or collaborative activities (e.g. thematic forums), on line events (e.g. virtual classrooms), games and exercises. All these resources contribute to support learner's activity to solve a problem or perform a task. Normally, a multimedia learning module is associated to a specific competence;
- *knowledge base*, composed of external knowledge resources web links, documents and reports coming from the knowledge management system or project management tool.

The overall Learning Base can be fed through traditional authoring tools used by the multimedia industry experts, but also through buying contents and modules on the market, or through allowing simple users (without any technological skills) to create directly knowledge and learning resources.

As for the **technological components**, besides the presence of a traditional Learning Management System integrated with a Knowledge Management System, Project Management System and an e-Business Suite, there are further innovative components represented by:

- an ad-hoc developed software layer, integrated with the overall architecture, that extends the LMS services and ensures the delivery of learning curricula according to the PBL methodology;
- a search engine that supports both taxonomy-based and problem-oriented searches;
- a virtual classroom that offers on line events and collaborative sessions, lectures, and brainstorming;
- a monitoring/reporting system that tracks the learners' activities and updates their competence profiles;
- a recommendation system that suggests PBL curricula according to the knowledge workers' competence profile, interests and skill gaps results;
- a multimedia delivery system, to manage the organization and delivery of multimedia resources.

Figure 3.4 shows the logical architecture of the Web Learning component that highlights: (a) the main learning processes it enables; (b) the typologies of available contents and (c) the technological components of the web based environment.

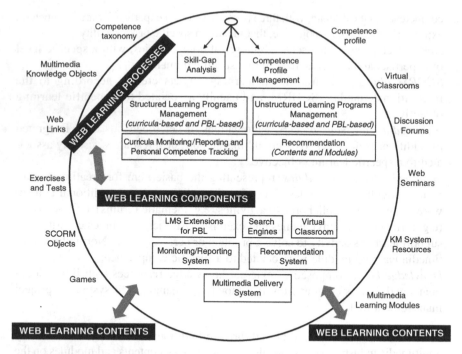

Fig. 3.4 The logical architecture of the web learning component of the "Virtual eBMS"

4.3.3 The Heterogeneity of Experiences Into the "Virtual eBMS"

Referring to the typologies of learning experiences enabled by the "Virtual eBMS", it is possible to identify six main categories, as illustrated in Fig. 3.5.

Specifically, a learner can access to *on-line web seminars* available through specific web applications. The seminars can be in real time, or recorded and stored into the knowledge base, in order to be used remotely later, in different occasions. Besides, a learner can also access to the same contents, but in off-line mode, through booking and taking an *interactive DVD* available within the media library.

Different and more complex usage concerns the access to *traditional web learning courseware*, constituted by a set of e-learning modules, with or without multimedia resources or interactive simulations, organized into a catalogue, and implemented according to SCORM standard.

Another different methodology to implement e-learning module is the one based on *PBL strategy*. Actually, according to this approach, a set of different and heterogeneous resources are available to the learners in order to support him in solving a problem or in performing a specific task. In this way learner can also interact with other learners, he/she can ask for suggestion to mentors and experts, he/she can access to discussion forums or virtual classrooms in order to share knowledge, experiences and ideas. The above mentioned modalities can also be integrated by

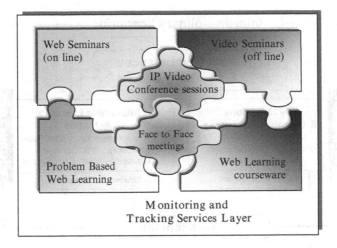

Fig. 3.5 Typologies of learning experiences enabled by the "Virtual eBMS"

videoconference sessions and *face-to-face meetings* that provide new opportunities for enriching the entire learning experience.

4.3.4 The "Virtual eBMS" Operational Framework for Designing PBL Curricula

A fundamental aspect for delivering high quality and effective problem-based learning curricula is the curriculum design phase.

Figure 3.6 shows the operational framework created within eBMS for the instructional design of problem-based curricula.

In particular, for interdisciplinary curricula, it's important to clearly define the target competences as well as the learning objectives that will be reached at the end of the learning experience. Moreover, a central stimulus that triggers the need to know and the direction of the learning is fundamental. Therefore, target competences and learning goals have to be opportunely framed into an interdisciplinary scenario that represents the overall planning context of the process. In this scenario, it is necessary to configure a complex business problem in order to stimulate and motivate learners in providing possible solutions integrating different disciplines.

The "operationalization" phase of the framework proposed evolves towards two complementary dimensions:

- the *cognitive dimension*, related to the knowledge acquisition process from the learner, and expressed through a set of key questions that stimulate learners in finding a solution;
- the *behavioral dimension*, related to the development of soft skills and attitudes for collaborative working and experiences, and expressed through a set of interactive

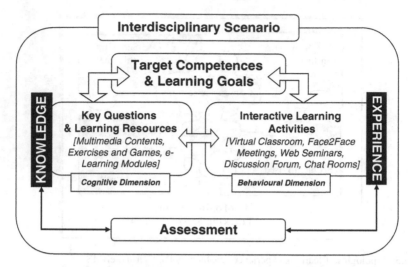

Fig. 3.6 The "Virtual eBMS" framework for PBL curricula design

learning activities that stimulate learners to practice knowledge and propose a solution. These activities can be real-time and recorded virtual classroom events, face-to-face events, web seminars, and collaboration services (forums, chat, shared workspaces and documents, team-project management, etc.).

Another key element of the model is represented by the identification of the most suitable learning resources for each knowledge domain which the curricula refer to. These learning resources are constituted by:

– a set of references (i.e. book chapters, web sites, presentations, papers, conferences, research centres, market trends, research projects, etc.);
– a set of multimedia learning contents (learning objects, presentations, images, simulations, etc.);
– a list of exercises and games.

Learning assessment and feedback close the model to verify the mastering level of the topics. Specifically, the final assessment consists in providing project deliverables that represent the solution proposed by learners, and/or the answer to some tests (i.e. multiple choices test, single choice test, open questions, matching questions, etc.). Project deliverables are "manually" evaluated by the mentors, while tests are "automatically" evaluated by the system.

The implementation of the operational framework contributes to create a stimulating context that motivates learners in performing a task, developing competencies, forming their own personality, developing self learning attitudes. These results are possible thanks to an effective implementation of the problem based approach, according to the guidelines given by Tchudi and Lafer, who describe good problems as having the following characteristics (Tchudi and Lafer 1996): (a) confuse just enough to provoke curiosity and provide a reason for learning; (b) provoke thought on new things in new ways; (c) help learners discover what they do and do not know; (d) ensure that learners reach beyond what they know; (e) create a need and desire for skill and knowledge; (f) naturally lead to interdisciplinary inquiry; (g) build strong communities of learners; and (h) lead to cooperation in the strongest sense that is based on the will and desire to succeed rather than a set of dictated behaviors that are advocated for the sake of politeness.

4.3.5   The Mentor Perspective for Implementing a PBL Curricula

Problem-based learning requires changes in the way teachers plan instruction, direct learning, transmit knowledge, oversee instruction, and assess learning (Torp and Sage 1998; Gordon et al. 2001; Maxwell et al. 2001).

In lecture-based instruction, teachers are in control and are the "experts" dispensing knowledge. In PBL, teachers select the problem, present it to the students, and then provide direction for student research and inquiry. Teachers behave as facilitators (mentors) stimulating the interactivity in all the learning activities, and the students are the main actors of the problem-solving process. Other tasks identified for mentors are: (a) keeping the learning process moving, (b) making sure that no phase of the learning process is neglected or misdirected, (c) probing the students' knowledge consistently and intently so that gaps in knowledge and reasoning are glaringly evident, (d) keeping all students involved in the learning process, and (e) guiding the group so that excessive stress is diffused while maintaining the challenge to learn without introducing boredom (Bayard 1994).

From the mentor's perspective, in order to create a PBL curriculum in the "Virtual eBMS" the following steps have to be performed:

1. definition of the *target competence* to reach and of the set of learning objectives which the curriculum refers to;
2. definition of the *key questions* associated to the specific problem, that represent a sort of learning guide for learners in finding the right solution to the complex problem proposed to them;
3. creation of the *multimedia knowledge objects*, by merging documents in their native format and by specifying the learning objective and additional references (see Fig. 3.7);
4. creation of the *tests* for the assessment phase;
5. classification of the *multimedia SCORM objects*, by using the same three-level competence taxonomy;
6. definition of the *complex problem* that learners have to face, and the description of the final solution to be provided;
7. identification of the *Web Links* to be used by learners as references to deepen some specific topics of the curriculum;
8. definition of the *exercises and games* for preparing learners to the final examination;
9. identification of the most suitable *learning activities* for learners, for practicing the knowledge acquired during the learning experience.

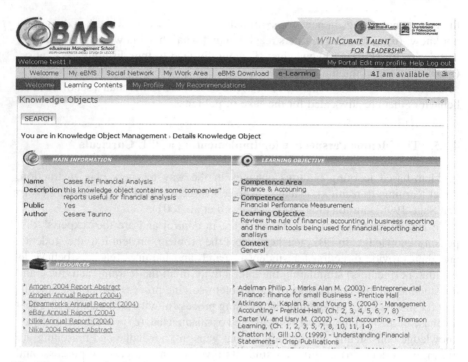

Fig. 3.7 An example of multimedia knowledge object

4.3.6 The Learner Perspective for Accessing to a PBL Curricula

Action learning approach relies on application (Barrows 1986) in which the learning link between cognition and action is genuine, pure and direct. Kolb defines learning as "a process whereby knowledge is created through the transformation of experience" (Kolb 1984a). Students learn through experience and active involvement. Considerable evidence supports the superiority of active over passive learning (Elam and Spotts 2004; Kayes and Kayes 2003).

This approach expresses the interactivity of learning that in the "Virtual eBMS" allows learners two different ways of accessing to the PBL curricula:

– well structured learning patterns;
– totally unstructured learning patterns.

In the case of *well structured learning patterns*, learners are immediately aware about the scenario in which their learning patterns are located.

When learners access to a PBL curriculum, a mentor introduces the learning scenario, the main target competencies and illustrates the problem they have to face.

In the case of *unstructured learning patterns*, the learner is free to browse the multimedia learning resource repository and to search and extract specific PBL curricula that can help him/her to solve the complex problem. Usually, this happens within the workplace, where "problems are ill structured, ambiguous, messy, complex, and most often do not have one correct answer" (Peterson 2004). The search of learning material can be performed by browsing the competence taxonomy, or by a launching a textual search.

In both cases, learners can specify the name of the curriculum, the problem that learners has to face, or a specific topic of interest. In this way, learners can access to the right portion of knowledge they need exactly when it is needed (Elia et al. 2006). Figure 3.8 shows an example of learner's access to a PBL curriculum.

In both cases (structured or unstructured learning patterns) a *recommendation system* operates in order to enhance the quality of the entire learning experience. Actually, it automatically searches for and suggests curricula to the learners, reasoning according to a complementary strategy:

- creating links based on a matching algorithm between the learner's competency profile and the module's competency profile;
- creating links based on a matching algorithm between the learner's interests profile and the module's knowledge domain.

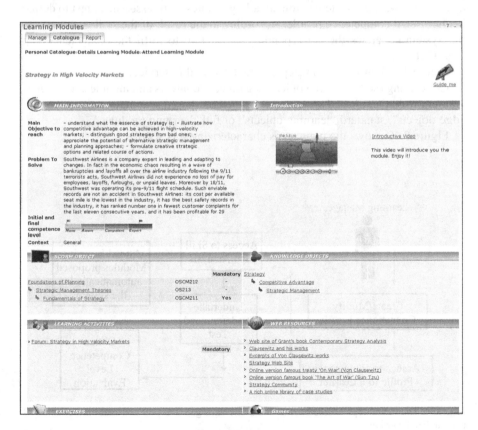

Fig. 3.8 Learner perspective of the "Virtual eBMS"

4.4 Personalizing Learning Process Through "Virtual eBMS"

Usually, the concept of personalization – which is based on individuals – may seem to contradict with the concept of community – which is based on groups.

Personalized learning, as well, enhances effectiveness of individual learners (Park and Hannafin 1993) and provides learners with opportunities to extend cognitive capabilities to managing the complexity of the learning situation (Xu et al. 2005). Additionally, personalization contributes to make more interactive a learning community, so enhancing its level of attractiveness.

In this perspective, "Virtual eBMS" offers a set of services allowing the personalization of the learning process, specifically:

– automatic skill gap analysis and real-time creation of personalized curricula;
– free search of learning objects, contents and modules;
– automatic recommendation of learning material.

As for the first service, it is based on the assessment tool that maps the learners' profile according to the competence profiles defined for them by the learning manager. In this way, the system automatically generates a pre-assessment test to define his/her initial competence profile. According to the result of the skill gap analysis, the system generates the corresponding curriculum to fulfil the competence gap (Assaf et al. 2009).

Figure 3.9 shows the main steps characterizing this service.

Concerning the free search of learning objects, contents and modules, it provides learners with a text-based search or a competence-based search to retrieve "knowledge objects", standard "learning objects" or full "learning modules".

Figure 3.10 shows the main steps characterizing this service.

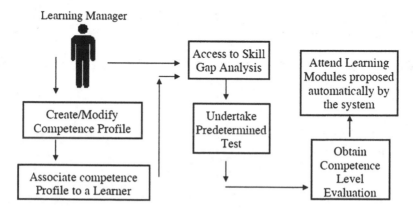

Fig. 3.9 The main steps characterizing automatic skill gap analysis and real-time creation of personalized curricula

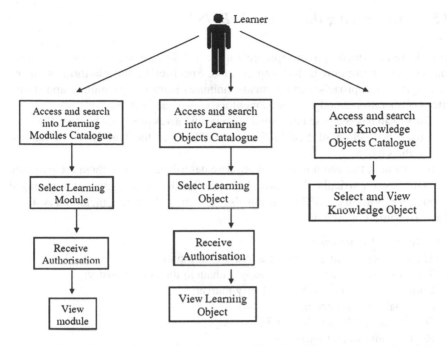

Fig. 3.10 The main steps characterizing free search of learning objects, contents and modules

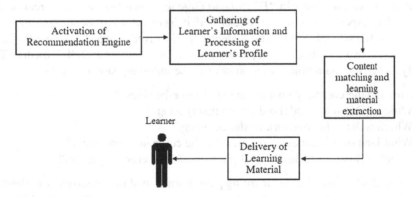

Fig. 3.11 The main steps characterizing automatic recommendation of learning material

Finally, as for the automatic recommendation of learning material, it proposes to learners a list of learning modules that match their interests or that can guarantee learners' competence updating and growth.

Figure 3.11 shows the main steps characterizing this service.

4.5   Experiencing the "Virtual eBMS"

The above described system represents a methodological and technological asset that enables innovation in learning process. Specifically, the platform, with the heterogeneous approaches and contents, animates learning community and stimulates collaboration among learners, mentors, experts and tutors.

The system has been used in several learning initiatives promoted by the e-Business Management Section of Scuola Superiore ISUFI, at the University of Salento (www.ebms.it).

In particular, two main initiatives are here described. Both of them are based on problem-based curricula that have been designed, implemented and managed through the "Virtual eBMS" (by using also multilingual version, including Arabic). The PBL curricula used are:

- e-Business fundamentals;
- The innovative management of a touristic destination;
- The innovative management of supply chain in the agro-industry;
- Competitive strategy in high velocity market;
- Financial performance measurement;
- Design and implement innovation strategy;
- Regional investment attraction.

Each of the above curricula has an average duration of 60 working hours.

The first initiative has been focused on *e-Business fundamentals*, and it was part of an International Master in *"Digital and Organizational Innovation"*, organised in 2007. The experience lasted 9 weeks and it involved 14 students coming from Morocco, Tunisia and Jordan. The students were involved in analysing the e-Business approach of five world-wide companies (eBay, eLance, Alibaba, Dell, Expedia). The analysis had the main objective to answer to the following key questions:

- How did the company take advantage from e-Business?
- Which e-Business model did the company adopt?
- Which is the value network of the company?
- What kind of e-Business processes did the company implement?
- Which e-Business technological platform did the company adopt?

Through this "inquiry-based" learning path, learners had the opportunity to develop the following subset of competencies characterizing the Business Engineer profile:

- to understand the role of internet to innovate the business model;
- to be aware about the advantage deriving from adopting e-Business within the companies;
- to identify and analyse the "candidate" processes to innovate through an e-Business approach;
- to choose the most suitable e-Business platform enabling communication and collaboration inside the company's value network.

During their experience, a lab technician and three tutors supported the learners for using the services and the multimedia resources of the web learning components of the "Virtual eBMS". Moreover, forums, chat rooms and virtual collaboration tools enabled sharing of documents and experiences with experts and mentors.

The learning assessment of this initiative was based on two main sources of data:

- the results of an "intermediate test" and a "final test", with automatic assessment performed by the platform through the usage of true/false questions, multiple choices questions, single option questions;
- a human-based assessment performed by the tutors and the mentors who evaluated the final project work delivered by the learners.

Table 3.2 shows the comprehensive results of the entire learning experience. As it is presented, the average final result is 3.7 over 5, and each test has a different weight for the calculation of the final result.

The second initiative has been focused mainly on contents related to the *innovative management of a touristic destination and of a supply chain in the agro-industry.* Specifically, the experience lasted for 1 month and it involved (in two phases) almost 30 managers of about 40 Tunisian companies operating within two industries. The main goal of this second experience was to sensitize and make aware the target about the benefits related to the e-Business and ICT adoption in tourism and agro-industry. The kick-off of the initiative happened during two different thematic workshops focused on the two specific themes and organized by the LINCET (www.ebms.it/euromed-tu.php) at the Technopole Elgazala, in Tunisi, respectively in May and June 2009.

After specific presentations about the e-Business usage and the Tunisian positioning in the digital economy, two e-Business platforms contextualized to the peculiarities of the two industries have been presented. Discussion and free questions from the companies representatives allowed to debate on the main topics of the workshops, and some interesting insights have been caught in order to initiate a personalized relationship with each participating company.

After each workshop, a presentation of the two on line PBL curricula has been done, and each participant received a free access for 1 month to the system and to the contents.

Totally, nine companies' representatives of agro-industry and 18 representatives of tourism companies used the free access for 1 month.

Through these two experiences, the two groups of participants had the opportunity to develop the following set of competencies, respectively referred to the agro-industry and tourism:

Table 3.2 Final results of the e-Business fundamentals curricula

	Intermediate test (min 0–max 5) (weight 20%)	Final test (min 0–max 5) (weight 50%)	Report (min 0–max 5) (weight 30%)	Total (min 0–max 5)
Average	3.53	3.36	4.37	3.70

- to be aware about the main trends shaping the industry, locally and globally;
- to identify the relationships between the different forces operating in the industry;
- to analyze the implications of ICT and e-Business on industry structure and competitiveness dynamics;
- to understand and choose the most appropriate e-Business solutions;
- to be ready for the implementation of a project to realize the transition from Business to e-Business configuration.

To evaluate the progress of their learning experience, a questionnaire has been defined and submitted at the beginning of the experience. The same questionnaire has been submitted at the end of the period, and the analysis concerned the comparison between the number of correct and wrong answers. During the month, a lab technician and three tutors assisted the companies in accessing to the system and in exploring the contents.

Figures 3.12 and 3.13 present respectively the learning progress of people participating to the initiative focused on the innovative management of a supply chain

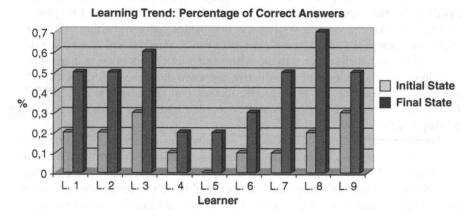

Fig. 3.12 Learning progress of the initiative focused on the innovative management of a supply chain in the agro-industry

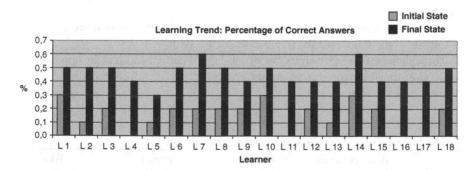

Fig. 3.13 Learning progress of the initiative focused on the innovative management of a touristic estination

in the agro-industry and to the initiative focused on the innovative management of a touristic destination.

5   Discussion and Conclusions

Stepien, Gallagher, and Workman provide the following interpretation of PBL (Stepien et al. 1993):

> *"Problem-based learning is apprenticeship for real-life problem solving ... students find a situation with undefined problems, incomplete information, and unasked questions. The scenarios presented to the students demand problem solving the way we find it in life: defining and detailing issues, creating hypotheses, searching for and then scanning data, refining hypotheses with the help of the collected data, conducting empirical experiments or other research, developing solutions that fit the conditions of the problem and evaluating and/or justifying their solutions so there is reason to expect conditions will improve."*

By combining the PBL methodology, learners can acquire the ability to learn quickly how to face and solve problems characterized by a growing level of complexity. As a result, people are empowered in problem solving since they acquire higher level of interdisciplinary competences and skills according to the level of complexity of problems. Moreover, since that problems are contextualized and referred to real business cases, learners are stimulated to search and organize the right information useful for determining the right solutions to complex problems.

Virtual eBMS embeds the PBL approach into a technological platform, so opening new scenarios in design and delivery of innovative learning environments. Its main characteristics can be summarized in the following ones:

- presence of tools for synchronous and asynchronous events;
- possibility to activate catalogue-driven and problem-driven curricula;
- integration between collaborative and self-pace approach;
- availability of tools for virtual and face-to-face meetings;
- openness to multi-source feeding strategy for content creation (authoring tools, on-the-shelf contents, built-in ad-hoc from knowledge management resources);
- contents and modules classification through a competence-based taxonomy.

These features make Virtual eBMS as a power tool that increases motivation for learning. Actually, learners are more motivated when they perceive they are acquiring new knowledge and skills, as well as when their educational activity is implicated in personally meaningful tasks.

As an illustrative application of the open networked "i-learning" model, Virtual eBMS is a proof-of-concept of *"interactivity"*, *"immediacy"*, *"internetworking"*, *"interoperability"*, *"interdisciplinarity"*, and *"individualization"*.

Interactivity is realized through many services and opportunities that enable collaboration, reciprocal exchange of knowledge and information, creating new spaces for socialization and participation. Also in contents, Virtual eBMS promotes interactivity that becomes visible in dynamic and hyperlinked contents, and in collaborative and ubiquitous services.

Immediacy is visible through specific functions and processes that ensure just-in-time interactions among learners and with the contents. A recommendation system selects and delivers to learners specific "learning pills", in a personalized way, in order to support his/her performance in the workplace.

Internetworking is the result of the interaction among learners in different communities and groups. Experts in several domains have the possibility to meet and to interact with other people, creating new relationships and new sources of ideas.

Interoperability, from a technological point of view, is a feature at the basis of the Virtual eBMS. It is the result of a great effort of integration among heterogeneous technological sub-systems, some of them coming from the market, and others created ad-hoc. Usage of international standards and shared technological choices allowed to create an integrated platform composed of many single interoperable components. The final result can be considered as generator of multiple learning contexts in which people belonging to different disciplines, with different backgrounds and cultures can inter-operate to solve a complex problem.

This last point opens the boundaries to the *interdisciplinarity*. Actually the analysis of a problem, the elaboration of possible alternatives and the choice of the solution depend on the capability to integrate different disciplines and know-how in one single holistic mindset, able to create multiple connections that conceptualize the final effective solution.

Individualization is another key dimension of the open networked i-learning model that is included in the Virtual eBMS. This characteristic is implemented to valuable represent the individuals within a community, but also to complete the personality of each individual by offering new opportunities to create new social and professional connections with other individuals.

Virtual eBMS represents an innovative learning community that mix effectively traditional learning with innovative approaches. In the next future, there will be a lot of similar learning environments that will gradually substitute the old e-learning systems. Education industry requires a lot of these innovation; they will contribute also to radically innovate the designers and the subject matter experts of the learning process, probably the most difficult aspect to innovate and the most critical issue to change.

References

Adelsberger, H., Bick, M., Körner, F., Pawlowski, J. M. (2001) Virtual education in business information systems (VAWI) – Facilitating collaborative development processes using the

Essen Learning Model. In: Hoyer H (Ed.), *Proceedings of the 20th ICDE world conference on open learning and distance education, The future of learning – Learning for the future: Shaping the transition.*

American Society for Engineering Education. (2009) *Creating a culture for scholarly and systematic innovation in engineering education. Phase 1 report,* available at www.asee.org.

Assaf, W., Elia, G., Fayyoumi, A., Taurino, C. (2009) Virtual eBMS: a virtual learning community supporting personalised learning. *The International Journal of Web Based Communities,* 5(2), 238–254.

Baets, W. R. J. (2003) *Virtual Corporate Universities,* Kluwer Academic Publisher, Norwell, MA.

Barrows, H. S. (1986) A taxonomy of problem-based learning methods. *Medical Education,* 20, 481–486.

Barrows, H. S., Tamblyn, R. (1980) *Problem-Based Learning: An Approach to Medical Education,* Springer, New York.

Bayard, B. (1994) Problem-based learning in dietetic education: a descriptive and evaluative case study and an analytical comparison with a lecture based method (Doctoral dissertation, University of Wisconsin, 1994/1995). *Dissertation Abstracts International,* 55, 1874.

Bovinet, J. W. (2000) Interdisciplinary teaching combined with computer-based simulation: a descriptive model. *Marketing Education Review,* 10(3), 53–62.

Brownell, J., Jameson, D. A. (2004) Problem based learning in graduate management education: an integrative model and interdisciplinary application. *Journal of Management Education,* 28(5), 558–577.

Collins, A., Brown, J. S., Newman, S. E. (1989) Cognitive apprenticeship: teaching the crafts of reading, writing, and mathematics. In: Resnick, L. B. (ed.), *Knowing, Learning, and Instruction: Essays in Honor of Robert Glaser,* Erlbaum, Hillsdale, NJ, pp. 453–494.

Dabbagh, N., Jonassen, D., Yueh, H. (2000) Assessing a problem-based learning approach to an introductory instructional design course: a case study. *Performance Improvement Quarterly,* 13(3), 60–83.

Dewey, J. (1938) *Experience and Education,* Macmillan, New York.

Elam, E. L. R., Spotts, H. E. (2004) Achieving marketing curriculum integration: a live case study approach. *Journal of Marketing Education,* 26(1), 50–65.

Elia, G., Secundo, G. Villani, P. (2001) Human capital as enabler of business innovation leadership. In: Romano, A., Elia, V., Passiante, G. (Eds.), *Creating Business Innovation Leadership,* Edizione Scientifiche, Napoli, Italiane.

Elia ,G., Secundo, G., Taurino, T. (2006) Towards unstructured and just-in-time learning: the "Virtual eBMS" e-Learning system, *Proceedings of Current Developments in Technology-Assisted Education,* Vol. 2, m-ICTE 2006, Seville, Spain, 2006, pp. 1067–1072.

Elia, G., Secundo, G., Taurino, C. (2009) The web learning system of "Virtual eBMS": a tool supporting unstructured and just in time learning. *International Journal of Networking and Virtual Organisations,* 6(2), 140–160.

Engel, C. (1991) Not just a method but a way of learning. In: Boud, D., Feletti, G. (Eds.), *The Challenge of Problem-Based Learning,* St. Martin's Press, New York, pp. 23–33.

Garvin, D. A. (1993) Building a learning organization. *Harvard Business Review,* 73(4), 78–91.

Gordon, P., Rogers, A., Comfort, M. (2001) A taste of problem-based learning increases achievement of urban minority middle-school students. *Educational Horizons,* 79(4), 171–175.

Hmelo, C.E. (2004) Problem-based learning: what and how students learn? *Educational Psychology Review,* 16(3), 235–266.

Hmelo, C. E., Ferrari, M. (1997) The problem-based learning tutorial: cultivating higher order thinking skills. *Journal for the Education of the Gifted,* 20, 401–422.

Kayes, D. C., Kayes, A. B. (2003). Through the looking glass: management education gone awry. *Journal of Management Education,* 27(6), 694–710.

Kilpatrick, W. H. (1918) The project method. *Teachers College Record,* 19, 319–335.

Kilpatrick, W. H. (1921) Dangers and difficulties of the project method and how to overcome them. Introductory statement: definition of terms. *Teachers College Record,* 22, 282–288.

Kolb, D. A. (1984a) *Experiential Learning: Experience as the Source of Learning Development,* Prentice-Hall, Englewood Cliffs.

Kolodner, J. L., Hmelo, C. E., Narayanan, N. H. (1996) Problem-based learning meets case-based reasoning. In: Edelson, D. C., Domeshek, E. A. (eds.), *Proceedings of ICLS 96,* AACE, Charlottesville, VA, pp. 188–195.

Leonard-Barton, D. (1992) The factory as a learning laboratory. *Sloan Management Review,* 34(1), 23–38.

Marquardt, M. J. (2002) *Building the Learning Organization,* Davies-Black Publishing, Palo Alto, CA.

Maxwell, N., Bellisimo, Y., Mergendoller, J. (2001) Problem-based learning: modifying the medical school model for teaching high school economics. *Social Studies,* 92(2), 73–78.

Meier, S., Hovde, R., Meier, R. (1996) Problem solving: teachers' perceptions, content area models, and interdisciplinary connections. *School Science and Mathematics,* 96, 230–237.

National Academy of Engineering (2004) *The Engineer of 2020: Visions of Engineering in the New Century,* available at www.nae.edu.

National Academy of Engineering (2005) *Educating the Engineer of 2020: Adapting Engineering Education to the New Century,* available at www.nae.edu.

National Academy of Sciences (2008) *Grand Challenges for Engineering,* available at www. engineeringchallenges.org.

Park, I., Hannafin, M. J. (1993) Empirically-based guidelines for the design of interactive multimedia. *Educational Technology Research and Development,* 41(3), 63–85.

Peterson, T. O. (2004) So you're thinking of trying problem based learning? Three critical success factors for implementation. *Journal of Management Education,* 28(5), 630–647.

Romano, A., Elia, V., Passiante, G. (2001) *Creating Business Innovation Leadership. An Ongoing Experiment: The e-Business Management School at ISUFI,* Edizioni Scientifiche Italiane, Naples.

Romano, A., Passiante, G., Petti, C., Secundo, G. (2005) Creating Human capital suitable for leading the XXI century organisations, *Proceedings of the 11th International Conference on Industrial Engineering and Engineering Management,* Northeastern University, Shenyang, China.

Sage, S. (2000) A natural fit: problem-based learning and technology standards. *Learning and Leading with Technology,* 28(1), 6–12.

Schmidt, A., Winterhalter, C. (2004) User context aware delivery of e-learning material: approach and architecture. *Journal of Universal Computer Science,* 10(1), 38–46.

Secundo, G., Passiante, G. (2007) Innovative practices in human capital creation: the eBMS case, *Proceedings of 28th McMaster World Congress, Hamilton Convention Centre,* Canada.

Secundo, G., Elia, G., Taurino, C., (2008) Problem-based learning in web environments: how do students learn? Evidences from the "Virtual eBMS Systems". *International Journal of Continuing Engineering Education and Life-Long Learning,* 18(1).

Secundo, G., Margherita, A., Elia, G. (2009a) Networked learning for human capital development. In: Romano, A. (Ed.) *Open Business Innovation Leadership,* Palgrave, London, UK.

Secundo, G., Margherita, A., Elia, G., Passiante, G. (2009b) A service science perspective to develop engineering systems professionals, *Engineering Education Global Colloquium, Budapest October 2009* organised by the American Society for Engineering Education (ASEE).

Senge, P. (1990) *The Fifth Discipline: The Art and Practice of the Learning Organization,* Doubleday Business, New York.

Stojanovic, L., Staab, S., Studer, R. (2001) eLearning based on the Semantic Web. In: Lawrence-Fowler W A., Hasebrook, J. (Eds.) *Proceedings of WebNet 2001 – World Conference on the WWW and Internet,* AACE, Orlando, Florida, pp. 1174–1183.

Tadmor, Z. (2006) Redefining engineering disciplines for the twenty-first-century. *National Academy of Engineering – The Bridge,* 36(2), 33–37.

Tchudi, S., Lafer, S. (1996) *The Interdisciplinary Teacher's Handbook: Integrated Teaching Across the Curriculum,* Boynton/Cook, Portsmouth, NH.

Torp, L., Sage, S. (1998) *Problems as Possibilities: Problem-Based Learning for K-12 Education*, Association for Supervision and Curriculum Development, Alexandria, VA.

University of Cambridge and IBM (2008) *Succeeding through Service Innovation: A Service Perspective for Education, Research, Business and Government*, available at www.ibm.com.

Vesper, K. H. (1973) A multidisciplinary experiment in management education, *Academy of Management Proceedings*, pp. 284–290.

Vest, C. (2006) Educating engineers for 2020 and beyond. *National Academy of Engineering – The Bridge*, 36(2), 38–44.

Ward, J. D., Lee, C. L. (2002) A review of problem-based learning. *Journal of Family and Consumer Sciences Education*, 20(1), 16–26.

Wright, B. T. (1999) Knowledge Management. Presentation at the Industry-University-Government Roundtable on Enhancing Engineering Education, May 24th, Iowa State University, Ames.

Xu, D., Wang, H., Wang, M. (2005) A conceptual model of personalized virtual learning environments. *Expert Systems with Applications*, 29(3), 525–534.

Chapter 4
Social Computing as *Next-Gen* Learning Paradigm: A Platform and Applications

Alessandro Margherita, Cesare Taurino, and Pasquale Del Vecchio

Abstract As a field at the intersection between computer science and people behavior, social computing can contribute significantly in the endeavor of innovating how individuals and groups interact for learning and working purposes. In particular, the generation of Internet applications tagged as web 2.0 provides an opportunity to create new "environments" where people can exchange knowledge and experience, create new knowledge and learn together. This chapter illustrates the design and application of a prototypal platform which embeds tools such as blog, wiki, folksonomy and RSS in a unique web-based system. This platform has been developed to support a case-based and project-driven learning strategy for the development of business and technology management competencies in undergraduate and graduate education programs. A set of illustrative scenarios are described to show how a learning community can be promoted, created, and sustained through the technological platform.

Referring to the six dimensions highlighted in Chap. 1, this chapter can be represented by the following radar.

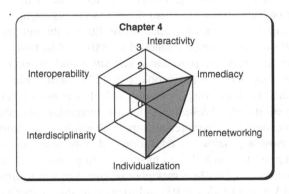

A. Margherita (✉)
Euro-Mediterranean Incubator – Department of Engineering Innovation,
University of Salento, Lecce, Italy
e-mail: alessandro.margherita@unisalento.it

G. Elia and A. Poce (eds.), *Open Networked "i-Learning": Models and Cases of "Next-Gen" Learning*, DOI 10.1007/978-1-4419-6854-8_4,
© Springer Science+Business Media, LLC 2010

Keywords Social computing • Web 2.0 • Social software • WeLearn • Case-based learning • Project-based learning

1 Introduction

The search of competitiveness pushes companies to leverage their hidden potential, by fostering new ideas, harnessing creativity, tapping the innovative attitude of employees and encouraging the proliferation of autonomy and entrepreneurship (Black and Porter 2000; Boyett and Boyett 2000). Leading organizations recognize human capital growth as a key value. Studies at corporate level show that high-performance competency development and learning processes return better results in terms of productivity, revenues and incomes (Brakeley and Meister 2005). These companies exhibit the distinguishing features of a learning organization (Garvin 1993) and many trends point to the commitment to lifelong learning and employee development (Meister 1998) as a new vehicle for creating a sustainable competitive advantage. In this perspective, success companies organize their human resource function to serve as a real "university", a trend also showed by the initiatives of leading companies like Cisco and Motorola.

The timeframe for learning has indeed evolved from schools to the whole life, giving rise to the importance of lifelong, life-wide, voluntary, and self-motivated pursuit of knowledge for personal and professional reasons (Commission of the European Communities 2006). This implies that there's today a need for effective strategies and tools to develop knowledge and competencies in people, both in "conventional" and non conventional educational institutions, initiatives and contexts.

The adoption of the Lisbon Strategy in 2000 has added new challenges for the European Union's member states to provide joint responses to such issues like ageing societies, skills deficits of the workforce and global competition. High quality pre-primary, primary, secondary, higher and vocational education and training become therefore fundament pillars for the success of organizations and countries.

Lifelong learning becomes a reality across Europe through the *Education and Training 2010* work programme (launched in 2001) and its follow-up, the *strategic framework for European cooperation in education and training* (in 2009) which identifies four long term strategic objectives: (1) making lifelong learning and mobility a reality; (2) improving the quality and efficiency of education and training; (3) promoting equity, social cohesion and active citizenship; (4) enhancing creativity and innovation, including entrepreneurship, at all levels of education and training.

However, most approaches to education and competence development are not properly addressed to reach those objectives. Many initiatives are still based on traditional methods inspired by a metaphor of knowledge as *transferable* commodity (Baets and Van der Linden 2003) and focused on the teacher as the key actor in the learning process. Self-organization ability of humans determines indeed the need to change the focus from a "teacher-centered" to a "learner-centered" approach where each individual can autonomously plan and carry on his/her own learning experience. The new paradigm is thus based on the assumption that a "mentor" guides the learner (more than student) through a "travel" in a terrain that needs to be explored. In this perspective, subject matters represent a set of experiences that each student can incorporate to develop his/her personality.

In the innovation process, the advent of web 2.0 and social computing has introduced a new paradigm in the ways how people communicate, with a special relevance for the generation of "digital natives", i.e. persons for whom digital technologies already existed when they were born, and hence have grown up with technology such as computers, the Internet, mobile phones and MP3.

Internet has always supported different forms of interaction (such as web seminars and online communities) but the web 2.0 represents an evolution in that it empowers end-users to build their own experience more actively, effectively, and in a collaborative way. In fact, "social platforms" and applications such as wikis, blogs, groups, podcasts, virtual worlds, social networking and social bookmarking are generating novel ways to acquire access, manipulate, process, retrieve, and visualize information. Respect to web 1.0, the social web has many distinguishing features, as showed in Table 4.1.

The potential of new technology can drive important innovations within human capital development. In fact, social media is dynamic, ubiquitous, real-time, collaborative and personalized and it can thus be a powerful enabler in the process of building competencies and skills in people. The challenge is to create innovative environments which allow a shift from time/place and content-predefined curricula to just-in-time/just in place and "on-demand" learning, and to harness the power of social computing to stimulate deeper approaches to learning and knowledge creation.

In this challenging endeavor, this chapter shows the development of a web 2.0 platform aimed to enhance open and collaborative learning. A new approach to developing personal skills through cases and applicative activities underlies the technological system. The strong integration of learning strategy and technology represents a potentially interesting feature of the experimentation here described.

The rest of the chapter is organized as follows: Sect. 2 describes the main theory background; Sect. 3 illustrates the design and development of the platform whereas Sect. 4 describes the applications made along with a set of illustrative scenarios. Finally, some discussions and conclusions are reported in Sect. 5.

Table 4.1 A comparison between web 1.0 and 2.0 (Source: Anderson 2007)

Web 1.0	Web 2.0
Data and information oriented	Knowledge oriented
Expert-generated	User-generated
Single-user oriented	Collaboration oriented
Software oriented	Service and content oriented
Exclusive intelligence	Collective intelligence
Publishing	Participation/editing
Database on the web	Web as a database
"All rights reserved"	"Some rights reserved"
Structured programming	Agile/extreme programming
Redesign/remake	Reuse
Single channel/device	Multi channel/device

2 Social Computing as Enabler of Learning

Social computing refers to using information systems as "places" for social interaction as well as spaces for data collection and manipulation. The field integrates social behavior and computer science and is thus found at the intersection of computer networks and social networks (Musser et al. 2003).

As a field, social computing has become more widely known because of the growing popularity of web 2.0 concepts and tools, the increased academic interest in social network analysis, and the rise of open source trend. In the weaker sense, social computing has to do with supporting social behavior through computational systems and is based on creating social conventions and collaborative contexts through the use of software. Thus, blogs, e-mail, instant messaging, social network services, wikis and social bookmarking illustrate ideas from social computing. In a stronger sense, social computing has to do with supporting computations that are carried out by groups of people showing the "wisdom of crowds", an idea popularized by James Surowiecki (2004). Examples of social computing in this sense include collaborative filtering, on-line auctions, prediction markets, reputation systems, computational social choice and verification games.

On the same line, the term "crowdsourcing" is positioned; it is referred to "the act of a company or institution taking a function once performed by employees and outsourcing it to an undefined (and generally large) network of people in the form of an open call" (Whitford 2007). This phenomenon is generating new business models based on openness, peering, and sharing of knowledge and ideas.

The shift of computing power from pure calculation to socialization and people-orientation has been also captured by leading institutions such as IBM and Microsoft which have created purposeful research centers on social computing whereas Forrester has started to use the term to describe next generation enterprise collaboration. Social computing platforms are characterized by capabilities such as: (1) support information about people, their preferences, communications and relationships; (2) create context of social networks around projects, teams and work groups; (3) provide an environment for social collaboration where people can share ideas, contribute knowledge and solve problems in unstructured socialization as opposed to rigorous workflows; (4) deliver content as a service accessible everywhere; (5) provide people-centric tools which allow interaction and empowerment.

The link between social computing and the emerging learning paradigm is evident: learning is more and more a networked rather than isolated and bounded process, with an increasing focus on experience and personality of people. Collaborative learning becomes a key theme and involves aspects related to pedagogy, sociology, communication, computer science and psychology. At different levels, collaborative learning processes are increasingly incorporated with the objective to promote active learning (Barkley et al. 2004), and collaborative networked learning is relevant to understand how knowledge workers change their mindset (Roschelle 1992), influencing one another and converging or diverging with respect to knowledge (Weinberger et al. 2007).

The ideal setting for collaborative learning is a learning community, i.e. a "social space" where to develop new insights and perspectives, a learning laboratory (Leonard-Barton 1992) where to enhance critical knowledge, skills, and judgment. The use of emerging learning technologies is a central aspect to consider and there is a pressing need for integrated and networked technologies serving the specific features and needs of lifelong learners (Koper and Tattersall 2004). Indeed, the diffusion of virtual communities and social networks represent major triggers of a transformation in the way (learning strategies and "processes") of developing in people those competencies and skills (the "product") required from the market.

Defined as "social software", given the capacity to have users develop web content in a collaborative way (Tapscott and Williams 2006), web 2.0 technologies such as blogs, wikis, podcasts, social bookmarking and RSS feeds can place learners at the centre of online activities and enable new ways of co-creating knowledge, collaborating and interacting.

Many of the studies done on the use of web 2.0 technologies in learning environments indicate how they positively support a collaborative learning paradigm, that leads to positive interdependence of group members, individual accountability, and appropriate use of collaborative skills (Parker and Chao 2007).

Web 2.0 promises to enhance collaborative work and skills development through direct involvement and experience of people, resulting in enhanced motivation and more dynamic communication than earlier. However, this (potentially) new generation learning paradigm has two big challenges to face: (1) to ensure openness and content reliability when applied for learning purposes (e.g. in institutional contexts); (2) to sustain the effective adoption and use by individuals and institutions.

This "user-generated" web allows actors to have a central role in the creation, editing and update of knowledge. Four applications are particularly relevant and diffused: (1) blog; (2) wiki; (3) folksonomy; (4) RSS. The term blog or web-log refers to a webpage containing brief paragraphs of opinions, information, personal diary entries, or links, called "posts", arranged chronologically in the style of an online journal (Doctorow et al. 2002).

A wiki is a webpage or a set of pages that can be easily edited by anyone who is allowed to access (Ebersbach et al. 2006). An easy-to-use online editing tool is used to change or even delete the content of a page whereas simple hypertext-style links among pages allow to create a navigable set of documents.

A folksonomy is a shared and evolving classification structure obtained as the result of the collaborative content tagging made by people (Specia and Motta 2007). Essentially, a folksonomy is a bottom-up, organic taxonomy that organizes content on the web (Tapscott and Williams 2006).

RSS (Really Simple Syndication) is a family of formats which allow users to find out updates to the content of RSS-enabled websites without actually having to go and visit the site. Information from the website (e.g. news and its synopsis, along with the originating website link) is collected within a "feed" and piped to the user in a process known as "syndication" (Anderson 2007).

Next section shows how the idea of social computing and the tools of web 2.0 have been integrated within a web-based architecture to support the creation of learning communities.

3 Building the Social Computing Space

The experience described in this chapter has been carried on at the e-Business Management Section (eBMS) of Scuola Superiore ISUFI (University of Salento) in the frame of a research project which involved also the University of Milan. The main objective was to develop a social computing space, later named "*WeLearn*", aimed to support different learning initiatives at undergraduate and graduate level. One key challenge was thus to take into account, at design level, the varying learning style, pace and competency development needs that normally characterize different learning communities.

It is of relevance to mention that the project has leveraged a 10-year experience accumulated at the eBMS in the design, implementation and experimentation of innovative web learning platforms (e.g. the "Virtual eBMS", awarded with the Brandon Hall prize in 2006).

Next sub-sections describe the technological infrastructure, the user profiles and learning processes enabled by *WeLearn*.

3.1 *Technological Infrastructure*

WeLearn was implemented as a web application built on *Drupal*, an open source Content Management System (CMS). This specific CMS was chosen after an extended benchmarking of several platforms available within the open source community. The choice was based on evaluating the following characteristics and dimensions: (a) presence of blog, wiki, folksonomy and RSS; (b) presence of user profile management service; (c) level of modularity, flexibility, and customizability; (d) presence of document management tools; (e) availability of components/modules add-ons; (f) accessibility to documentation and developers' guides; and (g) existence of multilingual support.

An initial screening produced a selection of five CMSs: Typo3, eZ Pubblish, Drupal, Joomla! and Wordpress. These systems were installed and evaluated by a mixed team of software developers, hardware specialists, curricula designers and e-learning experts. Based on several tests, the team agreed on the choice of Drupal for the good trade-off among easiness of use, overall functionalities, and customizability. The software infrastructure has been based on Apache web server using PHP software language, MySQL database. Some services have been developed and added to the standard suite through ad-hoc integration and customization, as for the 3D visualization of documents. Figure 4.1 shows the login page of *WeLearn* with the username and password boxes, the password request function and the welcome message.

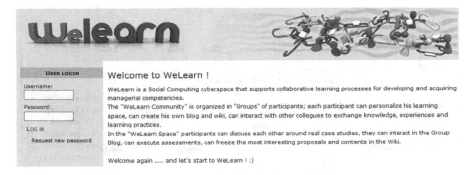

Fig. 4.1 Login page of *WeLearn*

3.2 *User Profiles*

Two main "profiles" of individuals have been identified as members of the community enabled by the platform. In particular, beside the traditional role of administrator as (technological) system supervisor and manager, *superpeer* and *peer* represent the key owners of learning processes arising within *WeLearn*.

The *superpeer* is a domain expert who acts as a mentor in that he/she stimulates the discussion and collaborative problem solving inside the community. The superpeer introduces a specific issue or topic and a real case which addresses that topic. Consequently, he/she proposes a problem to solve, uploads or creates documents and learning resources, evaluates the deliverables produced by learners, and acts a "social analyst" who analyses the dynamics of interaction among people within the community. If the superpeer leads the learner in the inductive exploration of new knowledge and the collaborative solution of problems, the *peer* is the learner who is motivated to develop a specific competence, also by interacting with other peers and the superpeer to solve a problem. The peer is thus stimulated to collaborate with the other members of the community in order to solve the problem and develop his/her own level of knowledge as related to a set of relevant competencies.

WeLearn is a web-based system and it can thus support learning processes arising among individuals located in distant places. In this perspective, peers and superpeers can also belong to different organizational contexts (e.g. companies, research laboratories and universities) and meet up in *WeLearn* because of a common interest in developing a specific competence or expertise.

3.3 *Learning Processes*

Five main activities build up the macro learning process within *WeLearn*: (1) community creation; (2) learning activation and scoping; (3) individual and collaborative working; (4) learning assessment; and (5) knowledge systematization

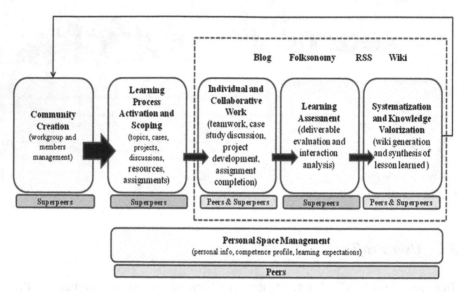

Fig. 4.2 High level learning flow within *WeLearn*

and valorization. A sixth underlying activity is the management of the personal space within the platform.

Figure 4.2 shows a high-level flow of the process which is described afterwards.

The first step is the *creation of the learning community* through the definition of a workgroup and its members. The composition of a group is typically made by a superpeer who "aggregates" members previously registered to the system. The criterion of aggregation is the participation to a common education initiative (e.g. a Master's on company performance and value creation) but members can also participate to different workgroups. This is a sign of the logic of openness and community building which underlies *WeLearn*.

Once a workgroup is defined, a superpeer *"activates" the learning process* by introducing a new topic (e.g. the *stakeholder value*) and a set of associated issues (subtopics and areas of discussion) as well as one or more real company cases (e.g. the stakeholders' report of Nokia). The superpeer challenges peers to solve a specific problem or realize a deliverable out of the learning process (e.g. a report on lessons learned from the case). At this purpose, he/she adds a new post on the community blog in which defines the kind of assignment submitted, illustrates the work to be done and all the details (i.e. delivery terms, modality of work, template to use, etc.).

The following step is represented by the *collaborative resolution of the problem/assignment*. The superpeer can require learners to work individually or suggest the composition of work teams. Besides adding new posts and comments, every peer can propose a new resource to the whole community (e.g. web link, video or research paper) potentially useful to solve the assignment. To reply to the assignment, peers can also use a template purposefully provided by the system according to the type of assignment (e.g. filling a table or using a map editor). Moreover, peers can use text-based search or the folksonomy keywords to retrieve content and resources existing within *WeLearn*.

Once the assignment has been completed and submitted, the superpeer starts the *assessment* phases. This process is executed "outside" the platform and is based on specific criteria defined by the superpeer who is asked to post a new message on the blog to detail the results of the evaluation.

The final evaluation is directly related with the last phase of the learning process, that is the enhancement of community knowledge through the *valorization of new knowledge* emerged in the discussion and collaborative resolution of the problem/assignment. Peers who turn out to be the best with reference to a specific assignment are invited to populate the community wiki with new entries related to the deliverable produced or other content generated (e.g. the best report on the Nokia case is added as a wiki page on the stakeholder value). However, since a distinguishing feature of any wiki is to allow everyone to create new contents or edit the existing ones, also in *WeLearn* every peer and superpeer is entitled to add new pages in the community wiki, regardless of the deliverable created.

Within the platform, all the peers create their own profile by providing personal and professional information, indicating the competences they aim to develop and their expectations from the participation to the community. The *creation and update of the personal space* can be made in all the moments of the learning process and existence of the community.

Naturally, the six activities described above represent a simplified schema for representing who makes what in platform. The life of a community is indeed typically made by integrated activities and learning processes arising among different teams and workgroups.

Next section illustrates the learning process and the experimentations made of *WeLearn* in undergraduate and graduate education initiatives.

4   *WeLearn* in Action: Applications and Examples

WeLearn has been applied in different education initiatives at undergraduate and graduate level, both in the academic world and in corporate settings. Three significant experiences are described hereafter.

The first experimentation was made (Oct 2008–Jan 2009) in a course on *Knowledge Management* (KM) held at the Faculty of Engineering of the University of Salento. The course is framed in the *Management Engineering* curriculum and involved 20 students (average age of 23 years) in a learning path focused on the emerging strategies, processes, metrics and technologies for managing and monitoring strategic knowledge within organizations.

A second context of application has been the *International Master's in e-Business Management* (IMeBM), organized by the eBMS (Apr 2008–Mar 2009). This initiative involved 23 graduated students (average age of 24 years) representing four

Southern Mediterranean countries (Egypt, Jordan, Morocco and Tunisia). The Master course aims at creating experts in the field of organizational and digital innovation enabled by the Information and Communication Technology (ICT).

Finally, *WeLearn* was used in the frame of FHINK, the International *Corporate Master's* in *Business Engineering* organized by the Italian Finmeccanica group (Oct 2008–Jun 2009). The Master involves 29 participants (average age of 25 years) representing 16 different countries worldwide. More than an academic program, the initiative is strongly targeted at developing competencies and areas of knowledge of specific interest for the company. The Master is thus a preliminary training phase for candidate employees of Finmeccanica.

Table 4.2 shows a synthesis of the three initiatives in terms of topic, education level and number of students involved.

It is evident that the audience and the learning objectives of these initiatives are quite different. However, the purpose of adopting *WeLearn* was very similar since the platform has been used to enable collaborative learning processes among participants through the creation of a virtual learning community. The expert/mentor (basically, the responsible of the course or module within the Master's) firstly introduced in class a topic and business world issue, and illustrated real life experiences under different points of view. After this "face-to-face" phase, community members started sharing ideas and knowledge and activated the learning processes described backwards.

Participants collaborated to exchange knowledge, solve problems, complete assignments, and develop personal competencies and skills in a peer and community-oriented learning environment. The objective was to eliminate traditional psychological obstacles and distances among "professors" and "students", resulting in a more efficient hybridization of collective experience and intelligence. The major role of superpeers was thus to feed interaction, answer questions, give suggestions and comments.

Figure 4.3 shows the home page of *WeLearn* after the login made by a superpeer of the IMeBM program.

As showed in the figure, the main functions/menus of the social computing space portal are: (1) traditional search function; (2) "search by keywords", which allows to use the folksonomy to retrieve, beside traditional search, documents, messages and other resources contained in *WeLearn*; (3) the user space (in the figure, *"amargherita"* is the username of the superpeer), with the access to the personal blog, community blog, portal statistics (recent hits, top pages and top visitors) and personal account;

Table 4.2 Contexts of application of *WeLearn*

Initiative	Topic	Level	Number of students
KM course	Knowledge management	Undergraduate	20
IMeBM Master's	e-Business management	Graduate/university	23
FHINK Master's	Business engineering	Graduate/corporate	29

Fig. 4.3 Home page of *WeLearn*

(4) the "e-club content", to create/add a new case study, assignment, group messages, blog entry or group video; (5) the "wiki", with all the pages created, the possibility to add new pages and verify recent changes; (6) "my task", including the work done, comments, navigation history and wiki pages created by the member logged in; (7) "my groups", i.e. the different workgroups in which the member participates;

(8) and "my network", with the list (and pictures) of all the members of the community, with the possibility to access directly to their personal profile or personal blog.

In the central frame, an interactive 3D animation is used to show the company cases contained in the platform.

Finally, the main menu on the top is made by the direct access to the "home" page and "assignment list", beside the traditional "log out".

A key moment in all the three initiatives was the submission of a case study to act as a catalyst issue for the learning process. Typically, a new case is added by the super-peer by compiling five sections: (1) background and company profile; (2) previous situation and issues; (3) actions and results; (4) lessons learned and managerial implications; (5) additional info and resources.

Figure 4.4 shows the template provided by *WeLearn* to insert a new case study (upper part of the figure) and how the case of Intel – *Leveraging Capabilities for Strategic Renewal* is visualized in the platform (lower part). Instead of creating ex-novo the description of the case, the superpeer can also upload a document (e.g. a pdf file) which contains the description of the case.

Strictly connected with the creation of a case is the submission of a problem or assignment to solve. As for the case study, also for the assignment the superpeer can use a template in which it is specified the name of the work, the type of problem (e.g. multiple choice, semantic map, "fill in the blank", etc.), the keywords for tagging, the referential case study (ideally, a given problem or assignment is defined with reference to a specific case study), some notes for the student (e.g. further sources to deepen topics such as web links, research papers, e-books, videos) and the due date for the work.

Figure 4.5 shows (in the upper part) the template provided and (in the lower part) the resulting blog post in which it is described the assignment.

It is important to remark that whatever new message or document added in *WeLearn* generates a feed RSS which allows to inform the whole community of the new resource available in the platform.

A particularly interesting assignment that the superpeer can submit for realization by peers is the creation of a *knowledge map* which synthesizes a specific domain, by linking together key concepts through relations. At this purpose, WeLearn provides editing features to allow such kind of graphic work.

Figure 4.6 shows how the students of the IMeBM "responded" to the assignment requested by creating a simple map which synthesizes the key concepts contained in a case study about Skandia.

When peers and superpeers add a new post or resource within *WeLean*, they are asked to "tag" their contribution by using a set of keywords already existing in the database or add new keywords necessary to describe the piece of knowledge added. In this way, it is possible to develop the bottom-up taxonomy or "folksonomy" which is dynamic and emergent (with a significant difference respect to predefined and top-down classifications which characterize traditional platforms).

Figure 4.7 shows an example of how the words "Knowledge Management" and "Organizational Learning" are used to tag a new blog entry. The most of the

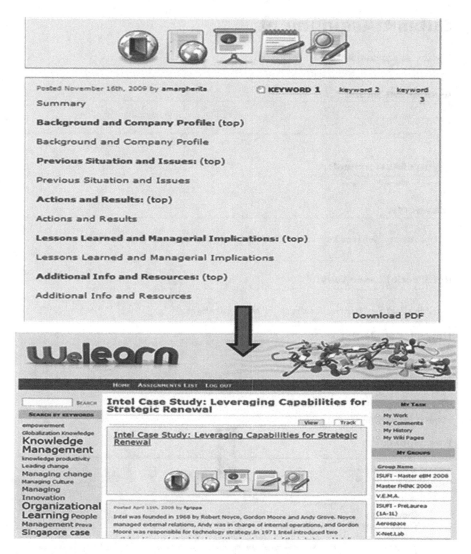

Fig. 4.4 Superpeer publishes a case study using the template

keywords are competence-oriented in order to facilitate the association of given pieces of information to competence development objectives.

Both the course on Knowledge Management and the modules held in the Masters' program have been concluded with a "systematization" of knowledge created. At this purpose, peers have been invited to contribute to the community wiki.

Figure 4.8 shows, in particular, a page on "e-Business Management" created by the fellows of the IMeBM.

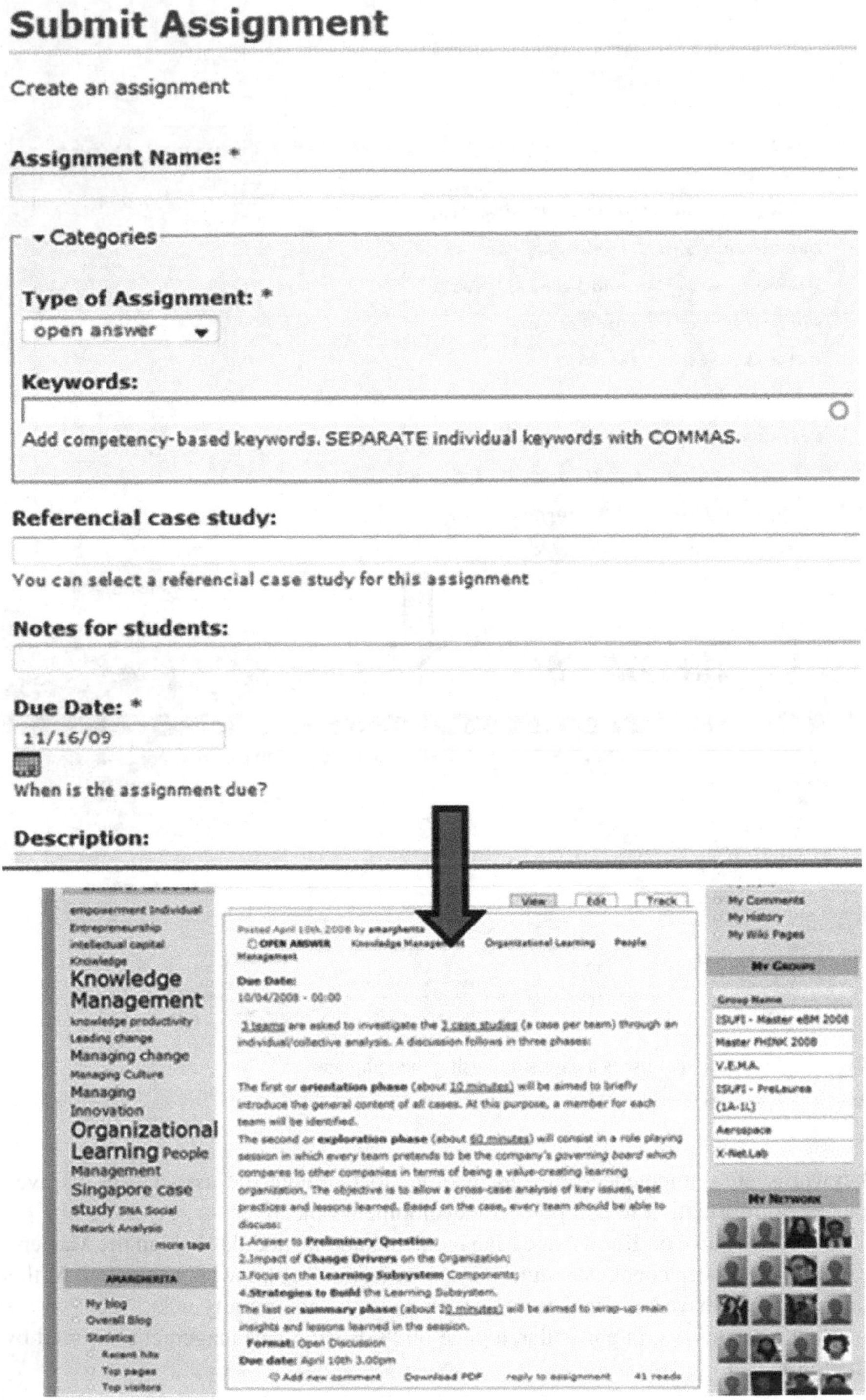

Submit Assignment

Create an assignment

Assignment Name: *

<hr>

▼ Categories

Type of Assignment: *

open answer ▼

Keywords:

Add competency-based keywords. SEPARATE individual keywords with COMMAS.

Referencial case study:

You can select a referencial case study for this assignment

Notes for students:

Due Date: *

11/16/09

When is the assignment due?

Description:

Fig. 4.5 Superpeer creates a new assignment

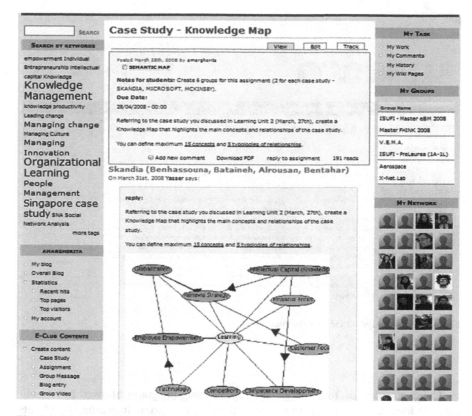

Fig. 4.6 Peers create a knowledge map

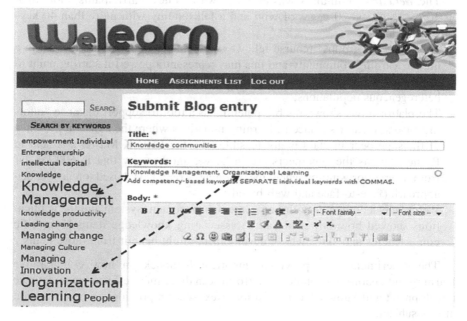

Fig. 4.7 Peers use the folksonomy

Fig. 4.8 A wiki page on e-Business management

The application of *WeLearn* in different learning programs allowed to consolidate the learning content and potential of the platform. Some interesting highlights are the following:

- The *WeLearn* community was enriched with 73 new participants, more than 30 case studies, 20 pages of wiki and a folksonomy with more than 40 keywords added;
- The different "groups" (course fellows and Master's students) are merged in a unique learning community and this may represent a powerful starting point to experiment the potential of knowledge and experience cross-fertilization within heterogeneous populations;
- The platform has shown his big potential as a tool to support distance "tutoring" and student assistance in learning initiatives where the constant presence of the superpeer in class is not feasible (e.g. the FHINK Master's is held in Rome whereas the superpeers are in Lecce, another city that is 600 km far from Rome) or simply when the learning strategy is based on a blended approach (face-to-face and web-based);
- *WeLearn* is a competence-driven content management system and the applications showed how powerful can be associating knowledge items to specific competencies and skills whose development might benefit from those items.

The experimentations provided important feedback on how collaborative learning and enabling technology platforms can drive more effective competence development and knowledge acquisition. Next section provides some discussion at this subject.

5 Discussion and Conclusions

WeLearn allowed to put in practice an innovative learning strategy within a new generation learning platform and can be considered as a response to the fast changing learning technology and actors we live nowadays. Interaction and social experience are critical issues in the conceptualization and design of collaborative learning environments. Social computing offers an interesting context for investigating new learning models based on principles such as openness, sharing and peer collaboration. In such new context, the teacher has a new role of "learning space creator" and facilitator providing continuous support to learners who participate with enhanced motivation through a learning experience which has a taste of discovery.

As an illustrative application of the "i-learning" concept (see Chap. 1), *WeLearn* is a proof-of-concept of *"interactivity"*, *"immediacy"*, *"inter-networking"*, *"interoperability"* and *"individualization"*.

First, *WeLearn* is an example of *interactivity*: blogs, wiki and RSS feeds allow to support real-time interaction among members as well as between members and the system. Besides, free access to member profiles, educational background and professional information may be the basis for establishing fructuous relations and collaborations for knowledge exchange, learning or working purposes.

Second, *WeLearn* is an example of *immediacy*: the platform is populated with knowledge items which can be applied just-in-time to solve specific problems or provide answer to given questions. The different blog posts and wiki pages contain indeed codified know-how (to be applied as it is), "tips & tricks" and contacts/references to access to the tacit knowledge possessed by the owner of that blog post or wiki page.

Third, *WeLearn* is an example of *inter-networking*: beside the use of the Internet as key infrastructure for connection, this aspect relates to the possibility to involve in learning processes several actors, with differentiated expertise and background. New opportunities are thus offered for collaborations and constructive comparison with other people, making *WeLearn* a powerful tool for creating networks of competencies and knowledge beyond traditional organizational and cultural boundaries.

Fourth, *WeLearn* is an example of *interoperability*: open source software used for building the platform permit integration with other services developed on purpose and other systems as well (e.g. human resource management systems, document management tools, multimedia repositories) through the use of open interfaces and technological standards.

Finally, *WeLearn* is an example of *individualization*: within the platform, a learner can ideally find his/her own dimension of professional growth though individual study and collaborative learning. In this sense, the community dimension does not prevail on the individual dimension as it's always possible to use the platform to deliver personalized learning paths and competence development initiatives, according to the interests and motivation of each learner.

In order to develop the professional skills and competencies required by organisations today, it's necessary to reflect more on people behavior.

Unfortunately, many education methods and initiatives still do not address this need. There is an increasing need to define guidelines for the design of environments which boost the benefits of collective intelligence and collaboration. In such endeavor, this chapter contributed by deepening the social aspects of learning to embrace experience in learning processes and to stimulate the creation of communities. Next research will be addressed to investigate the potential of virtual and immersive reality as hot trends which could drive a more intense integration among social communities and professional networks.

Environments like *WeLearn* will be more and more used in the next future both in academic and corporate contexts since they can speed up the process of knowledge and experience retrieval needed to better execute workplace activities. Social platforms like Facebook and Twitter attract more and more users who spend an increasing portion of their (spare?) time navigating, chatting and posting.

Professionals who are involved in the design and implementation of learning and training initiatives should probably take into serious consideration that, in the very next future, there will be no more boundaries between "what" and "when" is working, socializing and learning.

References

Anderson P (2007) What is web 2.0? Ideas, technologies and implications for education. *JISC Technology & Standards Watch Report.*

Baets W and Van der Linden G (2003) *Virtual corporate universities.* Kluwer, Norwell, MA.

Barkley E, Cross PK and Major CH (2004) *Collaborative learning techniques: a handbook for college faculty.* Jossey-Bass, San Francisco, CA.

Black SB and Porter LW (2000) *Management: meeting new challenges.* Prentice-Hall Publishers, New York, NY.

Boyett J and Boyett J (2000) *The guru guide: the best ideas of top management thinkers.* Wiley, New York, NY.

Brakeley H and Meister J (2005) Greater expectations: how corporate education can boost company performance. *Accenture Outlook Journal.*

Commission of the European Communities (2006) *Adult learning: it is never too late to learn,* COM(2006) 614.

Doctorow C, Dornfest F, Johnson JS, Powers S, Trott B and Trott MG (2002) *Essential blogging.* O'Reilly, Sebastopol, CA.

Ebersbach A, Glaser M and Heigl R (2006) *Wiki: web collaboration.* Springer, Berlin.

Garvin DA (1993) Building a learning organization. *Harvard Business Review* 73(4): 78–91.

Koper R and Tattersall C (2004) New directions for lifelong learning using network technologies. *British Journal of Educational Technology* 35(6): 689–700.

Leonard-Barton D (1992) The factory as a learning laboratory. *Sloan Management Review* 34(1): 23–38.

Meister JC (1998) *Corporate universities: lessons in building a world-class work force.* McGraw-Hill, New York, NY.

Musser D, Wedman J and Laffey J (2003) Social computing and collaborative learning environments, *Proceedings of the 3rd IEEE International Conference on Advanced Learning Technologies* (ICALT'03), Athens, Greece, July 9–11.

Parker KR and Chao JT (2007) Wiki as a teaching tool. *Interdisciplinary Journal of Knowledge and Learning Objects* 3: 57–72.

Roschelle J (1992) Learning by collaborating: convergent conceptual change. *Journal of the Learning Sciences* 2(3): 235–276.

Specia L and Motta E (2007) Integrating folksonomies with the semantic web. In Franconi E, Kifer M and May W (eds.), *The semantic web: research and applications*. Springer, Berlin.

Surowiecki J (2004) *The wisdom of crowds: why the many are smarter than the few and how collective wisdom shapes business, economies, societies and nations*. Anchor Books, New York, NY.

Tapscott D and Williams AD (2006) *Wikinomics*. Portfolio, London, UK.

Weinberger A, Stegmann K and Fischer F (2007) Knowledge convergence in collaborative learning: concepts and assessment. *Learning and Instruction* 17(4): 416–426.

Whitford D (2007) Hired guns on the cheap. Fortune small business. http://money.cnn.com/magazines/fsb/fsb_archive/2007/03/01/8402019/index.htm. Retrieved 2007-08-07. Accessed 01 December 2009.

Chapter 5
A Learning Dashboard to Monitor an Open Networked Learning Community

Francesca Grippa, Giustina Secundo, and Marco De Maggio

Abstract This chapter proposes an operational model to monitor and assess an Open Networked Learning Community. Specifically, the model is based on the Intellectual Capital framework, along the Human, Structural and Social dimensions. It relies on the social network analysis to map several and complementary perspectives of a learning network. Its application allows to observe and monitor the cognitive behaviour of a learning community, in the final perspective of tracking and obtaining precious insights for value generation.

The setting of the experimentation is a higher education community, framed within an International Master's program involving 23 learners from different Mediterranean Countries, interconnected in a community of students, tutors, mentors and external stakeholders.

Some preliminary results of this application confirm the assumption that knowledge is a social product, and recognize the importance of the social aspects of learning, valuing the role of collective and personal relationships as the levers for learning networks success.

Referring to the six dimensions highlighted in Chap. 1, this chapter can be represented by the following radar.

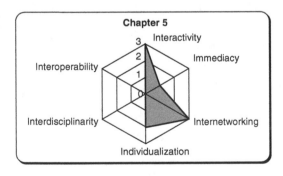

F. Grippa (✉)
Euro-Mediterranean Incubator – Department of Engineering Innovation, University of Salento, Lecce, Italy
e-mail: francesca.grippa@ebms.unile.it

G. Elia and A. Poce (eds.), *Open Networked "i-Learning": Models and Cases of "Next-Gen" Learning*, DOI 10.1007/978-1-4419-6854-8_5,
© Springer Science+Business Media, LLC 2010

Keywords Learning Dashboard • Open Networked Learning Community • Web 2.0 • Intellectual Capital • Human Capital • Structural Capital • Social Capital • Social Network Analysis

1 Introduction

Knowledge is a social product, built from the need to understand and solve problems (Vygotsky 1978; Johnson and Johnson 1996). In this perspective, learning has a social basis and many learners interact within the context of learning networks through collective and personal relationships. Among the different perspectives that emerge in literature recognizing learning and knowledge creation are social and cognitive constructs, Sfard distinguished between two metaphors of learning, i.e., the *knowledge acquisition metaphor* and the *participation metaphor* (Sfard 1998). The former represents a traditional view according to which learning is mainly a process of acquiring desired pieces of knowledge. In this view, the human mind is a container that is filled with knowledge structures and the learner is an owner of the knowledge constructed. On the other hand, the *participation metaphor* interprets learning as a process of participating in various cultural practices and shared learning activities, a process that structures and shapes cognitive activity in several ways. Accordingly, learning is seen as a process of becoming a member of community and acquiring the skills to communicate and act according to its socially negotiated norms (Lave and Wenger 1991). The participation metaphor provides a valuable insight into the role of learning networks in the process of knowledge creation. Despite these efforts of conceptualization, the value of learning networks still requires validation in a variety of contexts.

Networks have been explored at a large scale to study social inter-relationships over long periods of time (Degenne and Lebeaux 2005). For decades before virtual communities, Social Network Analysis (SNA) provided a mechanism to explore and describe complex relationships between individuals at all scales (Knoke and Kuklinski 1982). As a consequence of the variety of contexts in which networking has been examined, the terminology used to describe learning networks is complex; it is used to describe networks' functioning mechanisms and contextualization strategy in different fields.

Building on previous studies (Langan et al. 2007), this chapter proposes an operational model to monitor and assess an Open Networked Learning Community in Higher Education, investigating dynamics and value created by the communities. The model is based on a set of indicators organized according to the Intellectual Capital framework. This choice allows addressing Intellectual Capital measurement within a Learning Community. We present the case study of the International Master's Program in e-Business Management (IMeBM). For each student we collected data on project-related/business interactions, friendship network, technical support network, their score in the learning module, and their level of satisfaction.

2   Theoretical Background

Learning is one of the primary means through which individuals and organizations innovate and change. By learning we mean the acquisition and use of existing knowledge and/or the creation of new knowledge with the purpose of increasing the potentiality to produce desired results through reflection and experience (Senge 1990). Educational research and theory have long recognized that learning processes are socially situated and networked, and ideas are generated as a result of collective intelligence, efforts, and collaboration (Scardamalia and Bereiter 1994; Tharp and Gallimore 1988). The theory of *connectivism* stresses the importance of building networks and collaborative linkages to foster communication and dialogue (Siemens 2005). Siemens' theory builds on these ideas by conceiving learning as a process that occurs within multiple overlapping environments of dynamic core elements that support the *"amplification of learning, knowledge and understanding through the extension of a personal network"* (McLoughlin and Lee 2008).

2.1   Open Networked Learning: Definition and Approaches

A network is a system of connected entities, where a connection is something that allows one entity to send a signal to another entity, being an individual, a team or an organization (Becta 2007).

The metaphor of *"the network"* is seen by some researchers as the fundamental organizational form in learning environments. When networks are properly designed, they reliably facilitate learning to acquire competitive advantage for network nodes. This because through the process of interaction and communications *(learning by interacting)*, the entities that constitute the network will form a mesh of connections. Knowledge is embedded in this mesh of connections, and therefore, through interaction with the network, the nodes can acquire the knowledge. It is the organization of the network that supports learning, and if the network is designed appropriately, it will organize itself in order to best support learning. Network Learning is defined as learning by a group of organizations (Knight 2002). In this sense we intend "Network" as "Knowledge Network" or "Learning network" defined as *"a network formally or informally set up with the primary purpose of enabling any kind of learning to take place over the time for building capabilities eventually supported by the information and communication technologies"* (Romano and Secundo 2009).

The explosion of "Knowledge Network" or "Learning network" is an indicator of the individuals' need to contact and communication with other people, through the virtual learning communities or social space. Actually, searching for other people, often unknown but with a similar profile of interests, represents an interesting social phenomenon that offer new opportunities to communicate, to discuss, to learn. At this point, we can define Open Networked Learning as *"learning taking place in communities, social space, and other typologies of open environment without predefined boundaries, formally or informally set up, with the primary purpose of building capabilities eventually supported by the information and communication technologies"* (Romano 2009).

Instead of a learning theory focused on the learning processes of the individual, connectivism situates learning within the dynamics of social interaction, connection, and collaboration. Maintaining these connections is a skill that is essential for lifelong learning in a knowledge-based, networked society. Accordingly "cooperative learning" increases elaboration through higher-order thinking, meta-cognitive processes, and divergent thinking (Geer 2000). On the other side, the constructivist perspective presents interaction as a key success dimension of working against isolation. Even the behaviorists, though following a teacher-centered, structured approach, recognize collaborative interactivity as a way to reinforce group activity and rewards for learning.

The perspective of learning as a socio-dialogical process interprets the social dialogue as the best practice for creating learning communities able to develop different capabilities such as: (a) the recognition of plurality of ideas; (b) the sense of appreciation for different contributions to problem solving; (c) the awareness of multiple ways to see the world; and (d) the recognition of the importance of collaboration for both the team and the personal growth (Scardamalia and Bereiter 1994).

Other scholars (Geer 2000; Jonassen et al. 1999) illustrated the correlation between the social and the cognitive dimension of learning, highlighting the impact of social settings on the learning process as well as on the learning outcomes. In this perspective, the characteristics of a setting leading to productive learning become a central focus of interest in both social and cognitive theories. As Ruth Geer pointed out, traditional pedagogy has been quite clear about the physical or virtual place where socialization should take place that is "beyond the formalized structure of the classroom" (Geer 2000).

Wide evidence has been provided in literature about the effectiveness of collaborative learning environments enabled by advanced technology to support learning (King and Doerfert 1996). The emergence of the Internet technologies represents an important step in the evolution of the teaching and learning experience. At this purpose, collaboration among learners and between learners and tutors seems to increase significantly the learning potential of learners in an online environment (Aplin 2008). The most suitable setting for a fruitful learning experience appears the creation of *open, networked learning communities* where students establish and nurture relations within and across the communities' boundaries, involving internal and external stakeholders in their process of knowledge acquisition and personal growth.

Creating and supporting effective collaborative learning environments requires a process of identification of methodological frameworks able to monitor over time personal development and community's trends.

Since the open, networked community is recognized as an effective setting to facilitate the improvement of individual and team performance, many education programs as well as corporate training initiatives included the development of communities as part of the strategic process enabling competencies' growth. *Interactivity* can be considered as a fundamental aspect of learning process innovation inside a networked community. It encompasses the dynamicity of the nodes interaction in the usage of ICT and Internet-based tools. Besides, interactivity embraces also the presence of a collaborative (physical or virtual) community of people (and stakeholders), open to dialogue and interested in sharing and discussing valuable ideas. Flexible learning patterns built on the basis of learner's profile enhance the interactivity level of the whole learning experience.

2.2 Web 2.0 for Open Networked Learning Communities

The emergence of the web and the Internet technologies represent an important step in the process of evolution of the open networked learning communities, especially in higher education settings. Today learners need to process and to retain in a relatively short time an ever increasing quantity of information to update continuously their capacity to face real complex situations. They are supported by the innovative tools to develop their intellectual and creative mind and to boost the power of collaboration by creating virtual communities (Aplin 2008). This phenomenon is known as "internet-working", i.e., Internet is the underpinning infrastructure enabling distributed and collaborative working environments. Internet constitutes the "social" highway through which data, contents, knowledge and experiences flow.

In particular, Web 2.0 technologies have emerged to represent a valuable vehicle for more individualized learning system, mainly for their property of enabling processes of knowledge sharing, participated learning and continuous flows of ideas within and across the community (Delich 2006). Empirical research indicates how web 2.0 technologies in learning environments have the potential to support a collaborative learning process, that results in a positive interdependence of group members, future face-to-face meetings, individual accountability, and appropriate use of collaborative skills (Schaffert et al. 2006; Parker and Chao 2007).

Several case studies demonstrate the growing need of colleges and educational institutions to use social software to stimulate the active collaboration and create lively interactions between learners and mentors. The following Web 2.0 applications are emerging as tools able to meet the new needs of higher education:

- *Blogs*: the term blog refers to a webpage containing brief paragraphs of opinions, information, personal diary entries or links, called posts, arranged chronologically in the style of an online journal (Doctorow et al. 2002).
- *Wikis*: a wiki is a webpage or a set of pages that can be easily edited by anyone who is allowed to access (Ebersbach et al. 2006).
- *Folksonomies*: a folksonomy can be seen as a shared and evolving classification structure obtained as the result of the collaborative content tagging made by people (Specia and Motta 2007). A folksonomy is a bottom-up taxonomy that organises content on the web (Tapscott and Williams 2006).
- *Podcast*: a podcast is a multimedia file that is released to be downloaded through web syndication. This allows an automatic download of multimedia resources, that are automatically stored locally, on the user's computer or other device, ready to be used in off-line mode.
- *RSS (Really Simple Syndication)*: RSS is a family of formats which allows users to find out updates to the content of RSS-enabled websites. Information

from the website is collected within a feed (using the RSS format) and sent to the user in a process known as "syndication" (Anderson 2006).
- *Social Bookmarking*: social bookmarking sites allow the maintenance of a personal collection of links on line. Wikipedia defines social bookmarking as the capability to 'classify resources by the use of informally assigned, user defined keywords or tags'.

Several studies have shown that wikis and blogs can enrich classroom activities through up-to-date content development and active discussion that help learners achieve better scores and acquire new skills. Web 2.0 technologies support knowledge sharing processes that allow active learning within and across a community (Delich 2006). Web 2.0 may lead to a shift from a traditional teacher-centered perspective to a dynamic learner-centered approach.

This transition represents a profound change in the higher education sector. Web 2.0 technologies place learners at the centre of online activities, enabling new methods for content co-creation, collaboration and consumption. The challenging task for today's educational institutions is to find the most suitable way to integrate these tools in the classroom experience and in collaboration for distance learning.

A social constructivist paradigm has been used to explain the success of Web 2.0 applications, especially Wikis, in making the learning process more effective (Miers 2004; Higgs and McCarthy 2005).

Web 2.0 technologies also allow supervisors to monitor knowledge acquisition and knowledge sharing processes in all the learning phase, thus improving collaborative learning within and across the community. Blogs, wikis, podcasts, and RSS feeds place learners at the centre of online activities, enabling new methods for content co-creation, collaboration, and consumption, creating new ways of interacting to create new knowledge.

They place learners at the center of online activities and enable new types of collaboration and consumption, new ways of interacting with web-based applications. Blogs, wikis, podcasting, social bookmarking, RSS feeds represent "social software" able to support users to develop web content in a cooperative way (Tapscott and Williams 2006). So, social software contributes effectively in generating new interactive learning environment in which knowledge is co-created, and groups of people can collaborate, independently on their geographical position and time settings. Networks of communities arise, knowledge flows come up, dynamic links connect people, expertise and know-how. The Web becomes a no-boundaries place where the "inter-networking" takes shape and produces valuable results.

Furthermore social software tools are able to lead to positive interdependence of group members, future face-to-face meetings, individual accountability, and appropriate use of collaborative skills (Schaffert et al. 2006; Parker and Chao 2007).

If the effectiveness of the learning community finds a complete confirmation in literature, the shift from a traditional "closed" classroom context to an "open" community setting still needs to be investigated in terms of monitoring the community's boundaries and evolution. More integrated and holistic methods for assessing learning community growth are needed in order to measure the impact of learner-focused and community-based pedagogies (Palonen and Hakkarainen 2000).

To address this challenge, the following paragraphs of this chapter propose an operational framework to scan the individual and collective growth of a learning community, to discover drawbacks in the process of individual development and team growth.

2.3 Monitoring Learning Communities Through Intellectual Capital Measurement

Defined as a group of people sharing common values and engaged in learning together from each other (Goodyear et al. 2006), the "learning community" represents the real or virtual locus of the conversion of knowledge into a valuable asset, come to be known as an intellectual asset or Intellectual Capital (IC). Universities and other higher education institutions such as business schools need to consciously manage the processes of creating "their" knowledge assets and recognize the value of "their" IC to their continuing role in society (Rowley 2000). The entrenchment in traditional measurement paradigms represents in this sense a barrier to exploring the most interesting reason for measuring intangibles, i.e., learning (Sveiby 2004). Many practitioners suggested that IC consists of three elements (Sveiby 1997; Saint-Onge 1996; Bontis 1998), i.e., *Human, Structural* and *Social Capital*.

Human Capital includes knowledge, skills, and the abilities of people. It is a sort of combination between organizational and human capabilities for solving business problems. It also encompasses how effectively an organization uses its human resources as measured by creativity and innovation.

Structural Capital is the supportive infrastructure that enables human capital to work. It includes such traditional things as buildings, software, processes, patents, and trademarks. In addition, it includes also such things as the organization, organization's image, information system, and proprietary databases.

Finally, *Social Capital* represents the strength and loyalty of relations, which includes the connections that people outside the organization have with it.

If classification of components is mostly a shared subject, the intangible nature of IC makes the measurement a quite complex issue. The different measurement methods reveal a series of strengths and weaknesses that can be used as guidelines for the elaboration of innovative measurement approaches (Bontis 2001).

The Knowledge Assets classification (Marr and Schiuma 2001) describes Intellectual Capital as the sum of two categories of knowledge assets: Stakeholder Assets – divided into Stakeholder Relationship Assets and Human Assets – and Structural Assets – divided into Physical and Virtual Assets. As stated by the scholars, *"IC appears as an umbrella concept embracing the whole features and dimensions of intangible and knowledge resources"* (Schiuma and Carlucci 2007).

Several sets of qualitative and quantitative indicators have been presented (Bassi and Van Buren 2000; Edvinsson and Malone 1997; Van Buren 2001) to monitor learning programs developed by schools and to evaluate results in terms of knowledge, skills and competences acquired by people, as well as their successful position in the workplace. Concerning the monitoring of competencies acquired, an effort has been made to go beyond the traditional evaluation measures (e.g., training certificates, GPA) to consider the actual growth achieved by learners and aspects such as satisfaction, knowledge retention, and dynamics of relationships among schools and students. These measures share the limit of being carried out "ex-post", as they provide a static view of the quality of the intellectual capital generated within a community. They offer a picture of the knowledge assets and have difficulties in capturing the complexity of the value created by human interactions. In this perspective, Social Network Analysis (SNA) is an emerging method to complement the traditional ones to assess learning community performance. Social Network Analysis is *"a set of methods for the analysis of social structures, methods that specifically allow an investigation of the relational aspects of these structures"* (Scott 2004).

By investigating the deep pattern of interactions in a community, SNA might provide a set of techniques and metrics to be integrated in a new learning assessment dashboard. As shown by empirical studies (Penuel et al. 2006) although most of researchers consider gathering social network data to be problematic but feasible, still many scholars are concerned about privacy issues and the impact on the educational goals when data is shared with the learning community. This might be the reason why SNA is still not widely used within program evaluation (Durland and Fredericks 2006).

3 Experience in Action

Based on the literature review in the previous sections, this chapter presents the experiential background that brings to the operational model to monitor the degree of openness of a networked learning community, where individual and team level growth are integrated within the perspective of Intellectual Capital measurement. The experience described here is framed into the International Master's program in e-Business Management (IMeBM) organized by the e-Business Management Section of Scuola Superiore ISUFI (University of Salento, Italy). It involved 23 learners from Morocco, Tunisia, Egypt and Jordan, 15 tutors supporting the project work activities and 9 educational stakeholders involved in research projects. The students were physically located both in Italy and in their countries throughout the program's classroom and project work phases. Through a systemic and participative observation, the Master community's behaviour and cognitive activity (from March 2008 till January 2009) have been recorded. Periodically surveys have been also administered to collect further data and feedback, opinion, suggestions and satisfaction advices. A final web-survey was useful to know from the students the details of the external stakeholders they had met during the Master's Program.

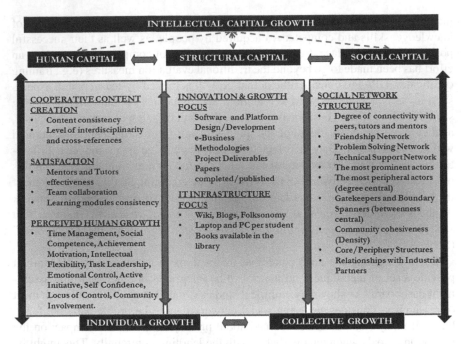

Fig. 5.1 A dashboard to monitor networked learning communities

4   A Learning Dashboard to Monitor Open Networked Learning Communities

In order to monitor the evolution of the networked learning community an operational model has been defined, to guide the analysis of trends and outcomes. As shown in Fig. 5.1, a dashboard has been set up, using the classification of Intellectual Capital based on Human, Structural and Social Capital. This dashboard is composed of a set of tools that help understand the evolution of the learning community along a continuum defined by the dimension "Individual Growth" and "Collective Growth". Some of these tools support the analysis of learners' satisfaction or skills like time management or motivation (individual growth); others, such as community cohesiveness or technical support network, help identify the growth of the group.

The three sections (with categories) that constitute the proposed dashboard are:

1. *Human Capital* section, to monitor the evolution of human capital looking at three main categories:

   – *Cooperative Content Creation.* This category provides an understanding of the ability to create knowledge in a collaborative way, either by developing a wiki or by sharing ideas and documents on the web 2.0 platform that students used. The evaluation of the knowledge acquired by students is operationalized by quantifying such variables as content consistency, level of interdisciplinarity, degree of deep investigation and presence of bibliographic references.

- *Satisfaction.* This category provides evidences on the quality of the learning environment in terms of collaboration, mentors' and tutors' effectiveness, quality of the learning materials, classroom logistics, learning module consistency.
- *Perceived Human Growth.* This category analyzes the psychological and behavioral factors that accompany the learners' developmental change. This category is based on the *"Life Effectiveness Questionnaire"* (Neill et al. 2003), thus it allows to observe and measure the desired changes of learning programs, and not only to record the appreciation or the assessment by the learners. Second, its scoring system is an important aspect of the tool's sensitivity to change. Third, it is able to recognize the stage of evolution of a wide range of life skills like self-confidence, proposition, communication, leadership, often promoted by educational programs, but hard to monitor in hybrid environment where the classroom is replaced by virtual community, workplace learning activities, and distance learning. The Perceived Human Growth category is based on the items described in Table 5.1.

2. *Structural Capital* section, to monitor the evolution of structural capital looking at two main categories:

- *Innovation and Growth Focus*, related to the development of innovative software, business methodologies, projects deliverables, research outcomes and awards received.

Table 5.1 Life effectiveness questionnaire (Neill et al. 2003)

Item	Description
Time management	Defined as an individual's ability to make efficient use of time
Social competence	Also referred in literature as Interpersonal Competence or Social Skills, it refers to the ability of an individual to function effectively in social situations
Achievement motivation	This scale assume that the more a person is motivated to achieve, the more likely it is that he/she will reach the objective he/she is trying to achieve
Intellectual flexibility	It refers to the individual's ability to appropriately adjust their views to accommodate the ideas of other people
Task leadership	It assesses people's ability to perform in a leadership role when there is a situational need
Emotional control	It aims to assess people's ability to deal with emotions under difficult or demanding situations
Active initiative	It is intended to capture the dynamic ability that is demonstrated by an individual who actively and independently initiates new actions and thoughts in a variety of personal and work settings
Self confidence	It is intended to provide a self-assessed measure of an individual's general self-esteem, self-efficacy and confidence of success in work and personal situations
Locus of control	It expresses the feeling of responsibility for the proper own action
Community involvement	It represents how much a person enjoys working with others

- *Infrastructure Focus*, to assess the infrastructure available for students. It is composed of the facilities and systems of the e-Business Management School in terms of technological equipment and education/research tools such as book and journal availability, as well as the social software tools.

3. *Social Capital* section, to monitor specific aspects like the degree of connectivity with external actors, but also the "friendship network", the "problem solving network" and the "technical support network". New profiles like gatekeepers or boundary spanners are identified and analyzed, as well as the emergence of clusters or cohesive sub-groups. Moreover, network evolution is also observed, looking at the external relationships that single learners developed, including on-site visits, telephone calls, possibility of future agreements.

Among the indicators of Social Network Analysis, the following ones have been used: *betweenness centrality*, *degree centrality* and *network density* (see Table 5.2 for a detailed description).

Table 5.2 Social network metrics included in the dashboard (Borgatti and Everett 2006; Wasserman and Faust 1994)

Level of analysis	Metrics	Description
Individual level	Actor betweenness centrality	It is the number of times an actor connects pairs of other actors, who otherwise would not be able to reach one another. It measures the extent to which a particular point lies "between" the various other points in the graph
	Actor degree centrality	It is the total number of other points to which a point is adjacent. It is also defined as the total number of a point's neighborhood. A point is central if it has a high degree, defined in the interval (0.00–1.00)
	Contribution index (CI)	CI is +1, if somebody only sends messages and does not receive any message. It is –1, if somebody only receives messages, and never sends any message. CI is 0, if somebody sends and receives the same number of messages
Group level	Group betweenness centrality (GBC)	The proportion of geodesics (shortest path between actors) connecting pairs of non-groups actors that pass through the group. GBC of the entire group is 1 for a perfect star structure, where one central person, the star, dominates the communication. GBC is 0 in a totally democratic structure where everybody displays an identical communication pattern
	Group degree centrality	It is the number of actors outside the group that are connected to members of the group
	Core/periphery structure	It is the extent to which a network revolves around a core group of nodes. This value can help to identify the presence of dense, cohesive core and sparse, unconnected periphery
	Density	The total number of relational ties (connections) divided by the total number of possible relational ties

Actor Betweenness Centrality is a measure of the potential for control of an actor who is high in "betweenness" if he/she is able to act as a gatekeeper controlling the flow of resources between himself/herself and the people connected to him/her.

Actor Degree Centrality is the property of an actor having a large number of connections with the other points in its immediate environment.

Density is a group indicator that refers to differing aspects of the overall "compactness" of a network and it represents the ratio between the total number of relational ties and the total possible number of relational ties.

Table 5.2 illustrates the set of indicators to monitor the learning networks evolution in terms of ability to evolve and create value.

The proposed model represents a learning dashboard to analyze the learning community growth at individual and group level, as well as to provide insights for the learning process itself. The assessment incorporates a variety of methodologies and tools: opinion surveys and satisfaction surveys, Social Network Analysis, brainstorming, personality and self-assessment tests. The dashboard is presented as a managerial tool to improve the overall learning experience in the community, by assessing individual and team growth.

5 Applying the Learning Dashboard to an International Master Program

In this section we present the main findings of the dashboard application to a case of learning community. We discuss the most interesting insights based on human capital, structural capital and social capital growth.

5.1 Human Capital Growth

Human capital was observed looking at three dimensions: satisfaction, cooperative content creation and perceived human growth.

– *Satisfaction*: Many students in the monthly questionnaires expressed their satisfaction for the way they collaborated with peers, which gave them the possibility to acquire new skills, like collaborative problem solving or managing conflicts within a team. They also appreciated the case-based and inquiry-based methodology that was at the basis of their education program.

In the opinion survey to investigate students' satisfaction, a student reported: "During my project work, I got the chance to learn from and collaborate with some of my mentors, who were all the time willing to explore with me new ideas and find out the best way to reach the best results. Their feedback and constructive comments on a timely manner resulted in significant changes and improvements of my project work".

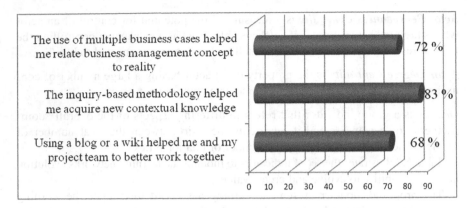

The use of multiple business cases helped me relate business management concept to reality — 72 %

The inquiry-based methodology helped me acquire new contextual knowledge — 83 %

Using a blog or a wiki helped me and my project team to better work together — 68 %

0 10 20 30 40 50 60 70 80 90

Fig. 5.2 Percentage of students who agreed with using blog and cases to create knowledge

- *Cooperative Content Creation*: To assess knowledge, skills and attitude developed within the community we collected data on individual and team performance (assignment scores, peers' evaluation, mentors' assessment). We also included indicators like the ability to collaborate in a team in order to co-create wiki content. Many students in the monthly questionnaires expressed their satisfaction with the way they collaborated with peers, which gave them the possibility of learning new skills, like collaborative problem solving, managing conflicts within a team. They also appreciated the case-based and inquiry-based methodology that underpinned their education program (see Fig. 5.2).

   As a Jordanian student commented during the survey: "*The use of new case studies and the possibility to work in team on research projects related to real business cases, helped me to learn how to apply knowledge to real situations. It also allowed me to apply the business management methodologies to my previous working experience.*"

- *Perceived Human Growth*: The majority of the students reported a high perception of development of their skills as monitored through the LEQ questionnaire (see Table 5.1). A Moroccan student during an interview was asked to refer to the connection between "wiki, blog and new technologies" and perception of "individual's ability to make efficient use of time". He stated that: "*It depends on the functionalities, on the Internet availability and on my time, because social life is not through the technology [...] in the reality, I like to discuss in face-to-face session rather than to write down in blog or wiki. I do think anyway that using a wiki and a blog helped me and my group manage our time in a better way*".

5.2   Structural Capital Growth

We looked at the evolution of the learning networks by exploring the degree of innovation created by the Master's students. Structural capital was observed in twofold dimensions: *infrastructure, innovation and growth* focus.

- *Infrastructure Focus*: in terms of the ability and willingness of students to use the Web 2.0 platform, after 8 months of classroom and project activities, we observed the following data:

  (a) A community wiki section has been populated and about 9 wiki pages have registered more than 350 reads in few months
  (b) Fifteen business case studies have been added by mentors and tutors
  (c) Fifteen different types of assignments have been submitted by mentors and tutors (mainly semantic maps and SWOT analysis)
  (d) Many comments, messages and knowledge resources have been tagged by both students and mentors and tutors. This has generated a folksonomy of about 40 keywords

- *Innovation and Growth Focus*: regarding this indicator we can describe the results obtained from the research project works in terms of the following results developed:

  (a) Thirty-five project deliverables in the field of Innovative management of e-Agrifood, e-Tourism, collaborative product design management and web learning
  (b) Software and pilot platform: a web learning course SCORM compliant on e-Business, the implementation and testing of several techniques for document clustering on PostgreSQL DBMS, a wiki on the topic of innovative management of new product development in the aerospace industry, and a pilot platform related to the integration of the SAP Business One with an already existing Digital Marketplace
  (c) Seven methodologies have been developed for: (1) process redesign to start up a Virtual Euro Mediterranean Academy; (2) business process evaluation in Model Driven Architecture; (3) sustaining the business value network in deciding about the distribution of complex design tasks between partners; (4) supporting the Small and Medium Enterprises in the adoption of the internetworked organisation paradigm; (5) sensitizing tourism decision-makers on the adoption and usage of ICTs and Web applications; (6) the analysis of the e-Business readiness of Jordanian private tourism operators; (7) business process reengineering within the agro-industry Supply Chain

The majority of the respondents (70%) had no technical problems in downloading multimedia files available on the web 2.0 platform. To the question *How much do you agree with this sentence "I was able to download different types of files without problems"*, some gave interesting comments, such as:

> "It depends on the Internet availability and on my time, because social life is not through the technology [...] in the reality, I like to discuss in face-to-face session rather than to write down in blog or wiki."

Almost all respondents (83%) agreed that the use of an inquiry and project-based approach to learning helped them retain more contextual knowledge and establish more fruitful contacts with other community's members. Many students (68%)

found very useful to use blogs and wikis to collaborate with peers, and many of them considered very important the discussion of real business cases (72%).

5.3   Social Capital Growth

The level of Social Capital has been analyzed looking at Learning Network and Social Network metrics. We extended the observation to the external boundaries of the networks. The survey results indicated that students were highly satisfied with the possibility to have access to the expertise of external members of the community. As a student reported: *"We had the opportunity to meet many professionals and managers such as the CEO of [...]. Being exposed to contextual experience and working directly on real projects helped me retain more easily concepts of e-Business that otherwise could have seem abstract".*

As shown by Fig. 5.3, at the end of the project phase, students had developed 165 new contacts in the business contexts they worked on: (1) tourism, (2) agro-industry, (3) aerospace industry. In Fig. 5.3 the value "New contacts" indicates people whom they met for the first time thanks to the project to which they were assigned (e.g., managers, IT specialists, CEO of partner companies). "Pre-collaborators" are external professors and managers of partner companies who had been introduced to students by the School, thus they were not completely new to the community.

The analysis showed that learners with larger external networks received higher marks for their classroom and project work activities. They also had a smaller network of friends to whom they would ask for help or support. For example, the most externally connected student reported to "rely only on three peers" within his friendship network to solve everyday problems.

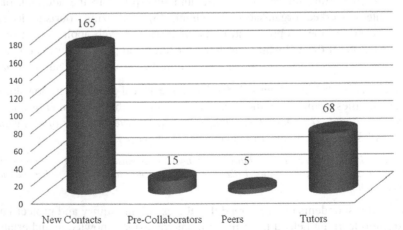

Fig. 5.3 Number of contacts developed at the end of the project work

The most connected actors to the external networks were the students who spent more time outside the school during their final project work.

The most connected learners were involved in tourism-based projects.

Figure 5.4a shows the social network of the most externally connected student. The square is an aggregation of stakeholders with the exception of the central node that represents the student. Each link means that there has been a business contact between the central node and external stakeholders. On the other hand, in Fig. 5.4b, each node is an actor, as no aggregation has been applied.

At the end of the Master's Program, this student developed 80 new business contacts. As shown by Fig. 5.4a, the student established 80 new contacts mainly with hotels and travel agencies, maintaining old relations with four stakeholders that were introduced to him by the tutors (see circle on the right of Fig. 5.4b).

Figure 5.5 shows the social network of the second most connected student, who mainly created new relationships with international software houses, hotels, research centres and travel agencies. In this figure, each node represents a set of individuals with whom the student (central node) communicated during the project work. The length of the ties is directly proportional to the intensity of communication between the student (labelled as "unknown" in Fig. 5.5, for privacy reasons) and the external actors. Each node is a cluster of actors grouped by company.

For example, the group of actors represented by the node "University" is the one that is communicating more frequently with the student. Other frequent communicators were actors working in "Hotels", "Research Centers", and "Travel Agencies". This is maybe due to the need of the student to look for materials for his Master's thesis, which likely could be found in academic/research institutions.

The Friendship Network is the densest of the three networks. It is composed of 138 ties connecting 39 actors (density = 0.0931). Only 38% of the 39 actors within the friendship network are Master's students, while the majority is represented by tutors, mentors, faculty members and PhD students. This insight is interesting as it provides evidence of the good degree of socialization within and across the learning community. The Technical Support Network is composed of 28 actors linked by 32 ties (density = 0.0423). Like in the Problem Solving network, (24 actors connected by 25 ties, density = 0.0453), also in this case there are different clusters represented by the IT support group and two clusters of students. The interesting insight emerging from this network is that only 9 people out of 28 reported that they would contact the School IT support team in case of problems. The majority of them would prefer solving the problem within their close friendship network.

6 Discussion and Conclusions

The chapter presents a learning dashboard to monitor the evolution and the value generated by a learning network composed of students, tutors, mentors and external stakeholders. It integrates the contributions of Intellectual Capital management in higher education environment with methodologies of social network analysis to

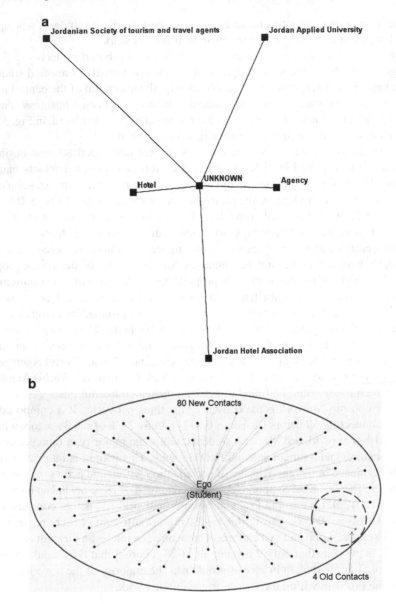

Fig. 5.4 (a) Ego-network of business contacts between the most connected student and stakeholders grouped by Institutions. (b) Ego-network of business contacts between the most connected student and stakeholders grouped by novelty of connections

evaluate the evolving nature of the learning network. At this purpose, an integrated model has been proposed, in which Learning Network growth is assessed by looking at the individual and team learning performance. Human Capital is evaluated in terms of learner's satisfaction and cooperative knowledge creation. Structural Capital is

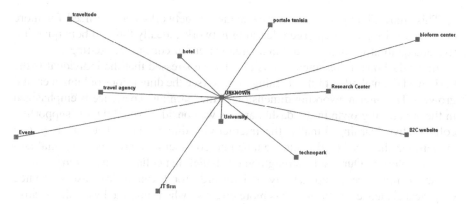

Fig. 5.5 Ego-network of business contacts between the second most connected student and external stakeholders

evaluated through the results developed during the project phases in terms of deliverables, software, methodologies and models developed by students. Finally, Social Capital is evaluated through methods of SNA investigating the frequency of new connections generated by students within and across their network's boundaries.

The preliminary results of this experiment indicate that learning networks possess the potential to harness greater efficiencies and greater capacities, at individual and team level. Highest performing students and team had developed extensive connections across the community's boundaries, and were also satisfied with the project-based approach followed during the Program.

This research reinforces the assumption that learning is not only an individual knowledge-acquisition process but also a process of participating in cultural practices and learning communities.

The methods and applications of Social Network Analysis provided with a new kind of relational information of the Master's students' participation. The SNA method allowed analyzing the external connectivity of the learning community, monitoring the new business contacts developed. Measuring the relations among participants of networked communities can help better understanding of the ways in which collaborative processes affect the individual students and the team growth.

Sociograms created through the use of SNA software tools are of great potential value for learning community mentors, who are responsible for instructional leadership and can apply SNA to assess the value of collaboration as a strategy for improving program outcomes.

The high number of links between students, mentors and tutors and the presence of multiple external connections developed by the high attaining students let us think that learners increased the value interacting in a dynamic way within and across the community's boundaries.

The dynamics of the observed interactions were consistent with mentor and tutor experiences and with students' scores. Learners interacted with multiple individuals during the project and internship stage.

This study highlights the complex nature of networks and the need for more detailed, exploration of emergent learning networks, ideally through both quantitative and qualitative methods and in a wide variety of educational settings.

In the dashboard presented in this chapter we stressed that the individual is the basic fundamental pillar of the learning process (see the dimensions of human capital growth). The inter-networking dimension of the learning experience is emphasized in the structural growth in the dashboard, as we consider Web 2.0 tools supporting collaborative learning. Finally, the interactivity dimension of learning is put in evidence in the dashboard while we take into consideration aspects like social networks evolution. Our results strengthen our belief that collaborative *interactivity* is a way to reinforce group activity and rewards for learning. We also presented empirical evidences that learning is more effective when supported via collaborative technologies that emphasize inter-networking and individualization.

The main limitation of this experience is represented by the small sample size and by the co-location of students during half of the Program. In case of students working always at a wide geographical distance, it would have been possible to monitor their communication looking at the amount of e-mails exchanges and obtain a fluid communication view of their dynamic relationships.

Future applications might include the integration of our network data with measures of individual personality, gender, country of origin, learning styles and attitude of students and tutors. It seems intuitive that networking behaviour should be affected by the personalities of the people involved.

References

Anderson P. (2006). 'What is Web 2.0? Ideas, technologies and implications for education', *JISC Technology & Standards Watch Report.*

Aplin C.T. (2008). Innovative trends in learning tools. *Journal of Cognitive Affective Learning*, Oxford College of Emory University, 4(2); 1549–6953.

Bassi L., Van Buren M.E. (2000). New measures for a new era, In Morey D., Maybury M. and Thuraisingham B. (eds) *Knowledge Management: Classic and Contemporary Works*, London: MIT Press.

Becta (2007). Emerging Technologies for learning. Chapter 2, Coventry, UK.

Bontis N. (1998). Intellectual capital: an explanatory study that develops measures and models. *Management Decision*, 36(2); 63–76.

Bontis N. (2001). Assessing knowledge assets: a review of the models used to measure Intellectual capital. *International Journal of Management Reviews*, 3(1); 41–60.

Borgatti S.P., Everett M.G. (1999). Models of Core/Periphery Structures, *Social Networks*, 21; 375–395.

Borgatti, S.P. and Everett, M.G. (2006) A graph-theoretic framework for classifying centrality measures. Social Networks 28(4); 466–484.

Degenne A., Lebeaux M.O. (2005). The dynamics of personal networks at the time of entry into adult life. *Social Networks*, 27; 337–358.

Delich P. (2006). Pedagogical and interface modifications: What instructors change after teaching online, Published doctoral dissertation, Pepperdine University, Malibu, CA, available at http://proquest.umi.com/pqdlink?Ver=1&Exp=09-09 2012&FMT=7&DID=1144195631&RQT=309&attempt=1

Doctorow C., Dornfest F., Johnson J.S., Powers S., Trott B., Trott, M.G. (2002). Essential Blogging, O'Reilly, Sebastopol, CA.

Durland M., Fredericks K.A. (Eds.) (2006). *Social Network Analysis in Program Evaluation: New Directions for Program Evaluation*, No. 107. Jossey-Bass, San Francisco.

Ebersbach A., Glaser M., Heigl R. (2006). *Wiki: Web Collaboration*, Springer, Berlin.

Edvinsson L., Malone M.S. (1997). *Intellectual Capital: Realizing your Company's True Value by Finding Its Hidden Brainpower*. Harper Business, New York.

Geer R. (2000). Social interdependence in collaborative interactivity in an internet based learning environment, Magill Campus University of South Australia, available at http://www.unisanet. unisa.edu.au/cccc/papers/non_refereed/geer.htm

Goodyear P., De Laat M., Lally V. (2006). Using pattern languages to mediate theory-praxis conversations in designs for networked learning. ALT-J. *Research in Learning Technology*, 14(3); 211–223.

Higgs B., McCarthy M. (2005). 'Active learning – from lecture theatre to field-work', in: O'Neill, G., Moore, S. & McMullin, B., (Eds) Emerging issues in the practice of university learning and teaching, Dublin, All Ireland Society for Higher Education [AISHE], 37–44.

Johnson D.W., Johnson R.T. (1996). Cooperation and the use of technology, *Handbook of Research for Educational Communication and Technology*, J. David ed., pp. 1017–1044.

Jonassen D.H., Peck K.L., Wilson B.G. (1999). *Learning with Technology: A Constructivist Perspective*, Merrill, Upper Saddle River, NJ.

King J.L., Doerfert D.L. (1996). Interaction in the distance education setting, available at http://www.ssu.missouri.edu/ssu/Aged/NAERM/s-e-4.htm

Knight L. (2002). Network learning: exploring learning from interorganisational networks. *Human Relations*, 55(4); 427–454.

Knoke D., Kuklinski J.H. (1982). Network analysis. Series in Quantitative Applications in the Social Sciences. London, UK: Sage University Papers, Sage Publications.

Langan A.M., Cullen W.R., Shuker D.M. (2007). Student networks and learning styles: a case study exploring investigative projects. Proceedings of the Science Learning and Teaching Conference, Keele University, June.

Lave J., Wenger E. (1991). Situated Learning: Legitimate Peripheral Participation. Cambridge: Cambridge University Press.

Marr B., Schiuma G. (2001). Measuring and managing intellectual capital and knowledge assets in new economy organisations. In M. Bourne (Ed.), *Handbook of performance measurement*, pp 1–30. Gee, London.

McLoughlin C., Lee M.J.W. (2008). The three P's of pedagogy for the networked society: personalization, participation, and productivity. *International Journal of Teaching and Learning in Higher Education*. 20(1); 10–27.

Miers J. (2004). BELTS or braces? Technology school of the future. Retrieved November 2006 from http://www.tsof.edu.au/research/Reports04/miers.asp

Neill J.T., Marsh H.W., Richards G.E. (2003). The life effectiveness questionnaire: development and psychometrics. Sydney: University of Western Sydney, available at http://wilderdom.com/ abstracts/NeillMarchRichards2003LEQDevelopmentPsychometrics.htm

Palonen T., Hakkarainen K. (2000). Patterns of interaction in computer-supported learning: a social network analysis. In B. Fishman and S. O'Connor-Divelbiss (Eds.), Fourth International Conference of the Learning Sciences, pp. 334–339.

Parker K.R., Chao J.T. (2007). Wiki as a teaching tool. *Interdisciplinary Journal of Knowledge and Learning Objects*, 3; 57–72.

Penuel W.R., Sussex W., Korbak C., Hoadley C. (2006) Investigating the potential of using social network analysis in educational evaluation. *American Journal of Evaluation*, 27(4); 437–451.

Romano A. (2009). *Open Business Innovation Leadership. The Emergence of the Stake-holder University*. Palgrave Macmillan, New York.

Romano A., Secundo G. (2009). Dynamic Learning Networks. Models and Case in Action. Springer, USA.

Rowley J. (2000). Is higher education ready for knowledge management? *The International Journal of Educational Management*, 14(7); 325–333.

Saint-Onge H. (1996). Tacit knowledge: the key to strategic alignment of intellectual capital. *Strategy and Leadership*, 24(2); 10–14.

Scardamalia M., Bereiter C. (1994). Computer support for knowledge-building communities. *Journal of the Learning Sciences*, 3(3); 265–283.

Schaffert S., Bischof D., Buerger T., Gruber A., Hilzensauer W., Schaffert, S. (2006). Learning with semantic wikis, Proceedings of the First Workshop on Semantic Wikis–From Wiki To Semantics, Budva, Montenegro, 109–123.

Schiuma G., Carlucci D. (2007). Knowledge asset value creation map – assessing knowledge asset value drivers using AHP. *Expert Systems with Applications*, 32(3); 814–821.

Scott J. (2004). *Social Network Analysis. A handbook*, SAGE Publications, Newbury Park, CA.

Specia L., Motta, E. (2007). Integrating Folksonomies with the Semantic Web. In *The Semantic Web: Research and Applications*, Vol. 4519/2007, pp.624–639, Springer Berlin/Heidelberg.

Senge P.M. (1990). *The Fifth Discipline: The Art and Practice of the Learning*. Doubleday, New York.

Sfard A. (1998). On two metaphors for learning and the dangers of choosing just one. *Educational Researcher*, 27(2); 4–13.

Siemens G. (2005). Connectivism: a learning theory for a digital age. International Journal of Instructional Technology and Distance Learning, 2(1). Retrieved December 11, 2005, from http://www.itdl.org/Journal/Jan_05/article01.htm

Sveiby K-E. (1997). *The New Organizational Wealth*, Berrett-Koehler, San Francisco.

Sveiby K-E. (2004). Methods for measuring intangible assets, http://www.sveiby.com/articles/IntangibleMethods.htm

Tapscott D., Williams A.D. (2006). *Wikinomics. How Mass Collaboration Changes Everything*, Portfolio First Edition.

Tharp R.G., Gallimore R. (1988). *Rousing Minds to Life: Teaching, Learning, and Schooling in Social Context*. Cambridge University Press, Cambridge, England.

Van Buren ME. (2001). Making knowledge count: knowledge management systems and the human element, http://learning.ncsa.uiuc.edu/ahrd/papers/VanBuren.pdf

Vygotsky L. (1978). Interaction between Learning and Development. In *Mind in Society*, Harvard University Press (pp. 79–91), Cambridge, MA.

Wassermann S., Faust K. (1994). *Social Network Analysis: Methods and Applications*, Cambridge University Press.

Chapter 6
Future Trends for "i-Learning" Experiences

Gianluca Elia and Antonella Poce

Abstract This chapter aims at shaping possible directions along with imagining the development and the evolution of the "i-Learning" paradigm. Specifically, three interdependent classes of future trends are depicted: technology-related trends and organization-related trends.

In technology-related trends, it is analyzed the strong contribution that emergent technologies can provide to innovate learning processes. In particular, Mobile Learning Environments (MLE) and 3D Learning Environments (3DLE) are described with more details. Moreover, it is analyzed also the role of the Future Internet framework (promoted by the EU in the VII Framework Programme) into the learning industry. Finally, innovative Personal Learning Environment (PLE) and Cloud Computing spaces are presented and discussed.

Referring to the organization-related trends, the model of the Stakeholder University is presented, discussed and analyzed. It is introduced as a new framework supporting competence development processes in twenty-first century, as an evolution of the traditional Training Departments, e-Learning Platforms and Corporate University archetypes.

Keywords Mobile Learning Environments • 3D Learning Environments • Future Internet • Personal Learning Environment • Cloud Computing • Stakeholder University • Learning Incubator

1 Introduction

In a recent paper published in October 2008 by the Economist Intelligence Unit (Economist Intelligence Unit 2008), the editorial team examines the role and the impact of technology in shaping the future of higher education. The results refer to a survey involving 289 executives, coming both from academic and corporate sides,

G. Elia (✉)
Euro-Mediterranean Incubator – Department of Engineering Innovation,
University of Salento, 73100 Lecce, Italy
e-mail: gianluca.elia@unisalento.it

G. Elia and A. Poce (eds.), *Open Networked "i-Learning": Models and Cases of "Next-Gen" Learning*, DOI 10.1007/978-1-4419-6854-8_6,
© Springer Science+Business Media, LLC 2010

mainly from USA (about 53%), and the other representing Europe, Asia-Pacific and the rest of the world.

Framed in a wider vision, the main findings of this study can be classified around two interdependent classes of interventions and trends: *technology-related trends* and *organization-related trends*.

In the *technology-related* class, we can set the results related to three pervasive and complementary phenomena: (1) the wide usage of mobile devices connected to pervasive wireless networks that are contributing meaningfully to realize an ubiquitous (in space) and permanent (in time) access to digital tools, multimedia resources, and digital social environments; (2) the growing of interoperability level across heterogeneous platforms that is opening new scenarios in rapid prototyping and software development; (3) the diffusion of new creative learning environments based on simulations, games, virtual reality, immersive environments, social networking applications and semantic web services.

In the *organization-related* class, we can include all the attempts moving towards the "hybridization" of learning through an open and stakeholder-based perspective, grounded on fruitful public-private partnerships and academic-corporate collaboration.

The following data from the Economist Intelligence Unit's report give a general overview of the above mentioned trends.

1. The main elements characterizing the evolution scenarios of higher education over the next 5 years are:

   - Searchable databases that complement campus libraries;
   - Creation of new areas of study born by the collaboration of universities with corporations and other third parties;
   - Complementarity between physical dimension and on-line dimension;
   - Integration between classroom and on-line experiences.

2. The main technological perspective characterizing the future scenario of higher education over the next 5 years are:

   - Online collaboration tools;
   - Software to support dynamic, individually paced learning;
   - Learning management systems;
   - Video and presentation tools.

3. The main organizational impact characterizing the future scenario of higher education over the next 5 years are:

   - A great number of interdisciplinary offerings;
   - An increasing of partnerships between universities and corporations;
   - Inter-university collaborations.

The above mentioned classes of interventions have to be strategically orchestrated and coordinated in order to meet and satisfy the following evidences highlighted by international organizations:

- Education and learning are the engines that fuel personal development, societal and economic progress. So, they represent hot topics that demand tangible and strong actions, synergistically designed and realized from academia, governments and private sector (Volkmann et al. 2009).
- Technological innovation (mainly Information and Communication Technologies – ICT) is radically changing educational and learning strategies, through proposing new models of production, distribution and access to web services and digital resources (European Commission 2008a).
- The major part of existing curricula in universities and business schools are not sufficient to prepare learners to face job challenges. The result is a huge number of people on the average skilled in few disciplines, but very weak in critical thinking, communication skills, mind flexibility, foreign languages fluency and international issues understanding. (Economist Intelligence Unit 2008).

The above mentioned three interdependent classes of interventions and trends are supported by several initiatives focused on ensuring quality and effective digital rights management.

Specifically, as for the quality, two interesting initiatives concern the European Learning Industry Group (ELIG) and the European Foundation for Quality in e-learning (EFQUEL). These initiatives contribute to the quality of e-learning as well as to the development of the educational systems as a whole.

As for the digital rights management (DRM), several technological and method-ological platforms used by big players (e.g., Sony, Apple, Microsoft, BBC, etc.) guarantee hardware manufacturers, publishers, copyright holders and individuals a secure and managed access to digital resources, contents and devices. Besides these systems, other emerging experiences have been arisen, such as the Creative Commons licenses launched in 2001, or the MIT Open Courseware launched in 2002 by the MIT, or the Open Educational Resources (OER) initiative launched in 2005 by the William and Flora Hewlett Foundation.

2   Technology-Related Trends

In 2008 the National Academy of Engineering (NAE 2008) published an interesting report about the grand challenges for engineering for the next decades. The challenges identified and described by the NAE derive from a deep reflection both on the technologies underpinning these challenges and on the main problems affecting today's and tomorrow's world. Next to the challenges related to making solar energy economical, to provide energy from fusion, to develop carbon sequestration methods, to provide access to clean water, to engineer better medicines, to prevent nuclear terror, to secure cyberspace, etc. there is also the challenge related to the enhancement of the virtual reality and the challenge related to advance personalized learning. This is a further confirmation that in the next decades the human capital development constitute a big challenge and, as such, it has to be deepen analyzed and transformed in a research agenda. Besides, since the common ground is represented by the technological progress, it is obvious to identify and to develop those technologies that can have a direct and indirect impact on the performance of the human capital development process and applications.

Two current phenomena that are introducing innovative features and that are opening interesting perspectives within the traditional learning contexts are represented by the *Mobile Learning Environments* (MLE) and *3D Learning Environments* (3DLE).

Actually, referring to the MLE, the mobility of digital technologies creates intriguing opportunities for new forms of learning because they change the nature of the physical relations between teachers, learners, and the objects of learning (Laurillard 2007). Moreover, mobile learning offers new chances for learning since it introduces profound changes in content design, content delivery, process monitoring, and interaction/collaboration dynamics, due to the following embedded characteristics (Laurillard 2007; Jones and Issroff 2007):

- It enables collaborative knowledge building by learners in different contexts;
- It enables learners to construct understandings and mindsets;
- It favors the changing of learning pattern and work activity;
- It allows the contextualization of the learning processes;
- It contributes to make more funny and enjoyable the entire learning experience.

Further insights related to the MLE come from the work of Gilly Salmon and Palita Edrisinga (Salmon and Edrisinga 2008) focused on the use of podcasting technologies to realize mobile learning environments. The authors, thanks also to the results coming from the IMPALA (Informal Mobile Podcasting and Learning Adaptation) project, observed a series of advantages for the use of podcasting in Higher Education, such as:

- Flexibility and learner control;
- Learner motivation and engagement;
- Cognition and learning;
- Novel way of presenting information and instruction;
- Learning locations;
- Fostering learning discussions;
- Contributing students;
- Accommodating "different strokes";
- Moving from entertainment to learning.

Referring to the 3DLE, Second Life is at the moment one of the most popular multi-user virtual world employed for educational purposes. Why should it be chosen as an educational setting? The answer is offered by Warburton who, studying the effectiveness of such a device, highlighted a series of reasons that makes educators approach it more and more frequently: *synchronicity, persistence, network of people, avatar representation and facilitation of the experience by networked computers* (Warburton 2009).

Trying to describe the distinctive characteristics of Second Life it is also important to state what Second Life cannot be assimilated to and this relates to its apparent similarity to multi-user dungeons and multi-player online games (MMOs), based, essentially, on role playing games.

Second Life is different because there is a substantial lack of a predetermined narrative or plot driven storyline:

"... social interaction exists not as a precursor to goal-oriented action, but rather, it occurs within an open ended system that offers a number of freedom to the player [...]. It is primarily this open-endedness, combined with the ability to create content and shape the virtual environment in an almost infinite number of ways, which has attracted educators to the possibilities afforded by immersive 3D spaces."

(Warburton 2009)

Second Life is increasingly used at Higher Education. Only in Great Britain three quarters of UK universities are estimated to be actively developing and using Second Life (Kirriemuir 2008). *The Beyond Distance Research Alliance* at the University of Leicester (UK) is currently carrying out a series of different research activities on the effectiveness of such a use and, according to researchers involved in the above analysis, results available seems comforting (http://www2.le.ac.uk/ departments/beyond-distance-research-alliance). The immersive nature of Second Life, crossing physical, social and cultural levels, responds to the need of living learning as an authentic experience to be more and more innovatively productive.

Table 6.1 below highlights the main features of 3D social worlds (Warburton 2009).

Other possible application fields of 3DLE that can potentially innovate the learning world are:

- 3D games (single-player or multi-player);
- Simulators (single-player or multi-player);
- 3D collaborative social environments;
- Role play games (single-player or multi-player);
- Virtual business games (single-player or multi-player);
- Social networking environments;
- Virtual Enterprise digital architectures.

By continuing in this investigation, we can consider the indications suggested by the Gartner Group in matter of top strategic technologies characterizing the next 3–5 years (where the term "strategic" indicates those technologies that have the potential for significant impact on the organization), we can reflect on those technologies identified in the survey performed in 2008 (Gartner 2008a) and 2009 (Gartner 2009a), and illustrated in Tables 6.2 and 6.3.

Moreover, a recent article published by the BBC (BBC 2008) identifies five breakthrough technologies for 2008, as illustrated in Table 6.4.

Developing the analysis of technology-related trends, and focusing on the education industry, it is now introduced the *hype cycle* of education technologies, an interesting and recent study carried out by Gartner (Gartner 2009b). The hype cycle, actually, is a term coined by Gartner (Gartner 2008b), and it is a graphic representation of the maturity, adoption and business application of technologies. Specifically, as shown in Fig. 6.1, a hype cycle is composed by five phases:

- *Technology Trigger*, the launching phase that creates significant enthusiasm and interest;
- *Peak of Inflated Expectations*, the "boom" of the first phase is blown out due to many failures and very few successful applications;

Table 6.1 A typology of 3D virtual worlds

Flexible narrative	Social world	Simulation	Workspace
MMPORGs (Massively multi-player online role-playing games)	Social platform, 3D chat rooms and virtual world generators	Simulations or reflections of the "real"	3D realization of CSCWs (Computer supported collaborative workspaces)
World of Warcraft, never winter nights, Ardcalloch	Second Life, Metaplace, Habbo Hotel, Sims online, vSide	Distributed observer, network google earth	Project wonderland, Olive, Open Croquet
The world is a setting in which your story or narrative unfolds within the constraints of the rules and goals set by the designers	The world may have elements of both a fictional and physical world and exists primarily as a place for social interactions to occur	The world is a close representation of the physical world and governed by the same rules	The world provides a virtual workplace setting for collaborative activity and often includes the necessary tools
You are a character in a role with a predefined purpose	You are an extension of yourself	You are yourself	You are yourself

Table 6.2 Gartner's top 10 strategic technologies in 2008

Top 10 strategic technologies	Description
Multicore and hybrid processors	New generation of chipsets that are bringing processor speeds in retail computers up and up (8 cores processors are just around the corner)
Virtualization and fabric computing	Hybrid environment in which different operating systems and applications run at the same time, with a real time management of hardware resources
Social networks and social software	Open and collaborative environments promoting social relationship, exchange of knowledge, experience and ideas
Cloud computing and cloud/web platforms	A new paradigm of computing that will be definitely part of our future. We will not necessarily be hosting our information and applications on one computer or device, but rather in the clouds – over the internet or whatever process follows – and are thus accessible via our work computers, home computers, personal devices and all over
Web mash-ups	A combination of many web services to create a new and more useful and valuable application
User interface	Next generation of interfaces based on interactive and multi-sensorial features. In this perspective the mouse will be soon obsolete, and replaced by touch screens (e.g., iTouch and Microsoft Surface)
Ubiquitous computing	Pervasive computing that interests not only "traditional" objects like PCs, PDAs, mobile phones, but also fridge, washing machine, heating system. This generates the Internet of things, that work and communicate each other, also autonomously, to perform a task and execute a job

(continued)

Table 6.2 (continued)

Top 10 strategic technologies	Description
Contextual computing	A multi-facets behavior of traditional devices that changes according to the context in which it is situated. This introduces proactivity to the devices, making them more "intelligent"
Augmented reality	The real-world reality augmented with technology and obtained through the overlapping of different data layers (geo-position layer, multimedia layer, virtual layer, etc.). The result can be visualized with a new generation mobile device or with a PC with a web-cam
Semantics	The ability of search engines and applications to understand what you are talking about, what is the context in which you are asking for some information, what is the real aim of your questions. This ability will enhance our capacity to get the work done quicker and more effective

Table 6.3 Gartner's top 10 strategic technologies in 2009

Top 10 strategic technologies	Description
Cloud computing	A style of computing that characterizes a model in which providers deliver a variety of IT-enabled capabilities to consumers
Advanced analytics	Analytical tools and models to maximize business process and decision effectiveness by examining alternative outcomes and scenarios, before, during and after process implementation and execution
Client computing	A new ways of packaging client computing applications and capabilities, enabled by virtualization
IT for green	The use of IT to greatly enhance an enterprise's green credentials, such as the use of e-documents, the reduction of travel through the promotion of tele-working and virtual meetings, the use of analytic tools to reduce energy consumption in the transportation of goods
Reshaping the data center	A pod-based approach to data center construction and expansion. This means the design of the entire site, but only the building of what is needed in the short-medium term, with evident savings of the operating expenses that can be invested in other fields
Social computing	A multiple use of social software and social media in the enterprise and in the participation and integration with externally sponsored and public communities
Security-activity monitoring	A new concept of security that is not based on prohibitions and restrictions, but on real-time monitoring and identifying patterns that would have been missed before, potentially critical and malicious
Flash memory	A kind of memory that is much faster than rotating disk, but more expensive, even if this differential is shrinking. It is moving up to a new tier in the storage echelon, offering a new layer of the storage hierarchy in servers and client computers that has key advantages including space, heat, performance and ruggedness
Virtualization for availability	The movement of a running virtual machine (VM), while its operating system and other software continue to execute as if they remained on the original physical server. This is obtained through replicating (also on-demand) the state of physical memory between the source and destination VMs, optimizing resources, cutting costs, lowering complexity, and increasing agility as needs
Mobile applications	Personalized applications, accessed through mobile devices, that realize a rich environment for the convergence of mobility and the Web

Table 6.4 BBC's five breakthrough technologies for 2008

Five breakthrough technologies	Description
The web to go	Represents a category of tools blurring the online and offline worlds. Actually, they provide offline functionality for web applications, with the immediate synchronization when an Internet connection becomes available (e.g., Google Gears, Adobe Air or Microsoft Silverlight)
IPTV	Identifies the television over Internet protocol. Actually this category of services has been hampered in the past because broadband speeds were not fast enough to deliver a reliable service. Nowadays, thanks to the wide diffusion of optical fiber and the new generation of ADSL connection (e.g., ADSL2+ that has a download speed up to 24Mbps), the IPTV is rapidly getting market shares (e.g., BT and Virgin Media)
Mobile VoIP	Represents a class of technologies that allow users to make cheap phone calls over the Internet, and mainly to have in a single logical repository the integration between data and voice. Mobile VoIP services and applications support currently the traditional mobile phone system (e.g., Skype, Nokia), in the perspective to become an enabling technology supporting new value added services that exploit the integration between databases and voice streams
Ultra mobile PCs (UMPC)	A new kind of mobile PC that is in the middle between a PDA and a traditional laptop or notebook. UMPC is not so diffused for its high price and poor battery, but the new generation of UMPC (e.g., Asus EEE and Macbook) have replaced the hard drive in favor of flash memory. In this way, thanks to the big innovation in flash memory field (e.g., Samsung flash memory reach 128 GB of storage capacity), the new UMPC can have a low weight (lower than 1 kg), an accessible price and good performance. These qualities are at the basis of the big diffusion of the UMPC that will characterize the next months
Wimax	An emerging wireless technology thatsan deliver high speed broadband over long distances. Some wireless players are boosting Wimax (e.g., Sprint and Intel) in the perspective to guarantee high quality of ubiquitous access. At the same time, Wimax represents also a breakthrough technology that can leapfrog the wired connection in the developing countries, offering a higher quality of services

- *Trough of Disillusionment*, the most critical phase since the technologies are completely abandoned and criticized for their failures;
- *Slope of Enlightenment*, a hide phase in which some businesses continue to experiment and understand the benefits and the value brought by a technology, creating and documenting new success stories;
- *Plateau of Productivity*, the phase in which a technology demonstrates the benefits of its application and usage, in order to be widely accepted and adopted, according to the needs and opportunities of a specific niche or entire markets.

Referring to the education industry, the hype cycle created and published by Gartner includes for each phase some key technologies, like:

- *Technology Trigger: business process outsourcing education* (delegation of an IT enabled business process to a third party that owns, administers and manages the

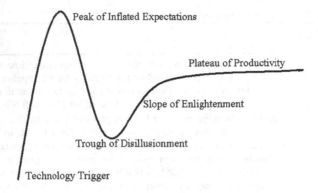

Fig. 6.1 A generic hype cycle of a technology, according to Gartner interpretation

process according to a defined set of metrics and interfaces), *mobile learning application* (heterogeneous learning services like collaboration and project work, educational games, real time feedbacks, e-books, that are accessed both through low-cost devices and more capable handsets supporting web browsing and Java platforms), *social learning platform* (extension of traditional Learning Management System with social software features supporting formal and informal learning activities), *e-textbook* (content can be edited and up-to-dated by including other contents of external sources, personal notes or multimedia assets).

– *Peak of Inflated Expectations*: *lecture capture and retrieval tools* (to capture, tag and retrieval lectures through a synchronized access to video, audio, materials and applications), *virtual worlds* (virtual environments in which participants are immersed in a 3D virtual space), *web based office productivity suites* (collection of applications used individually or collaboratively, that do not require delivery and maintenance from the adopter organization), *unified communication and collaboration suites* (integrated systems that merge workplace desktop applications with telephony and network services).

– *Trough of Disillusionment*: *mash-ups* (lightweight presentation layer integrating multi-sources contents and applications, generally to offer a new service through the usage of widgets, snippet and APIs), *e-learning repositories* (digital repositories for sharing learning material), *cloud e-mail for higher education* (no-fee e-mail services offered by big ICT market players to educational institutions), *podcasting learning content* (audio recorded material notified through RSS and delivered through a variety of portable devices).

– *Slope of Enlightenment*: *social networking in education* (web environments where individual information is aggregated, presented and shared in the perspective to create networks of people who can communicate and collaborate to share ideas and create new knowledge), *digital right management* (methods and systems to prevent unauthorized access and use of digital resources), *wikis* (collaborative system for creating and maintaining dynamically hyperlinked collections of web pages), *open source e-learning applications* (educational e-learning

systems developed via open source models and communities), *grid computing* (using computers own by several organizations to collectively accomplish large tasks like complex simulations).
- *Plateau of Productivity*: *web services for administrative applications* (applications that facilitate the internal integration and extra-institutional collaboration to perform education administrative functions).

The above presented studies allow us to reflect on the future trends of education related technologies. The reflection is further stimulated by the *"Future Internet"* initiative launched by the European Commission in the VII Framework Programme, and specifically in the ICT Key Research Challenge 1 named *"Pervasive and Trustworthy Network and Service Infrastructures"*, that is part of the Cooperation Programme. Future Internet provides an overall framework in which the main technological trends can be positioned.

It has been proposed in the awareness that the current Internet may in the long term not be fully capable of supporting the ever larger set of usages, constraints and requirements that it will have to face as it further penetrates our immediate surroundings and environment (some EU statistics give an estimation of 4 billions of Internet users in the next coming years).

So, the Future Internet aims to investigate a number of technological domains, as well as associated policy domains, that have a bearing on the network and service infrastructure elements of the Internet of tomorrow (European Commission 2008b). Specifically, the Future Internet initiative highlights six specific and highly interlinked objectives:

- *The Network of the Future*: aimed to shape "a network of networks" that will support a wide variety of nomadic and mobile interoperable devices, innovative services, ICT tools and applications, content formats and delivery modes. A new generation of telecom infrastructure, network and internet technologies will be used in the coming years as fundamental building blocks, supporting every real life contexts.
- *The Internet of Services*: representing a vision of the Internet of the Future where organisations and individuals, through virtualisation technology, can find software as services on the Internet, combine them, and easily adapt them to their specific context. Cloud computing is a model for enabling convenient, on-demand access to a shared pool of these configurable computing resources and services, designed and deployed according to SOA (service oriented architectures) principles.
- *The Internet of Things*: a visionary idea based on the fusion of man and machine, coupled with the explosion in machine intelligence and rapid innovation in ICT and other advanced technologies such as sensors and nanotechnology. The result is an Internet that connects not only computers and people to one another, but also that connects computers to things and things to things, thus creating an "Internet of Things".
- *Trustworthy ICT*: a horizontal aspect that respects citizens' rights and protects their privacy and personal data. The ambition is to coherently address security, trust and privacy from a technological, economic, legal and social perspective,

in an effort to ensure innovation and economic growth in a society providing freedom and security for its citizens.

– *Networked Media and 3D Internet*: shaped by the media convergence, thanks to which all kinds of media including text, image, 3D graphics, audio and video produced can be distributed, shared, managed and consumed through various networks, like the Internet, be it via fiber, WiFi, WiMAX, GPRS, 3G and so on, in a convergent manner. At the same time, advances in audiovisual technologies such as Digital Cinema and 3D processing increase the level of immersion and the quality of the experience, but also give rise to innovative applications, notably in gaming technologies and in virtual worlds.

– *Future Internet Experimental Facility*: inspired to the research and experimentation principles, through the creation of a multidisciplinary research environment for investigating and experimentally validating highly innovative and revolutionary ideas for new networking and service paradigms. This environment is continually fed by experimentally-driven research, joining the two ends of academic-driven visionary research and industry-driven testing and experimentation.

Figure 6.2 provides an overview of the Future Internet framework, as reported within the EU VII Framework Programme web site, in the ICT section (http://cordis.europa.eu/fp7/ict).

After so great, profound and multiple views about future technological scenarios that will influence and affect (directly or indirectly) the education industry in the next years, we would like to try to create an overall picture that can drive some important decisions in choosing and implementing an education technologies strategy.

At this purpose, we would like to stress the importance to "contextualize" the learning process. Actually, the *context* represents a dynamic reality that provides

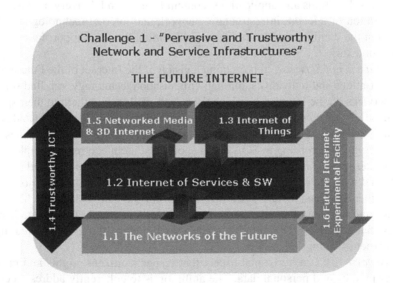

Fig. 6.2 The Future Internet framework in the EU VII Framework Programme

meaning to the information, so generating new interpretation and knowledge through a virtuous combination between physical/geographical locations and digital information (Van't Hooft 2008). So, the context becomes a sort of "mental state" that crosses real world physical places and virtual world digital spaces, whose boundaries are getting increasingly blurry.

In addition to the context, two other interdependent elements are *access* and *mobility*:

- *Access* is the condition to be "always on", in permanent and ubiquitous way, using every sort of integrated devices, portable applications, shared resources and pervasive networks;
- *Mobility* is the capacity to use and interact with heterogeneous and remote resources, during the physical movement from one place to another one.

Two final fundamental features that can be deducted by previous analysis are *user control* and *rich experience* (Van't Hooft 2008):

- *User control* reveals in the state to place the control in the hands of the user and provide ample opportunities for personalization, regardless of the organization he belongs to, and the content he is interested in;
- *Rich experience* reveals in the capability to access, aggregate, create, customize and share digital information in a variety of media formats, anywhere and anytime, and regardless of the platforms.

Thanks to these five characteristics, it is possible to envision a *Future Internet based educational framework* that can inspire the technological design of new learning environments. The five characteristics act as five levers to control, merge, activate and integrate the technological pillars and the IT enabled layers of the overall architecture:

- *Internet of Services*: focused on shaping and creating a cloud of user-oriented services that can be easily offered, combined and personalized from organizations and individuals.
- *Internet of Things*: focused on shaping and creating a web of relationships integrating human beings, machines and physical things that embed sensors and nanotechnology.
- *Internet of Contents*: focused on shaping and creating an integrated architecture of contents, made up of heterogeneous format and media, supporting multilingualism, involving many domains, integrating database of information, complex knowledge sources, unstructured knowledge bases and structured learning repositories.
- *Semantic Layer*: focused on shaping and creating a semantic backbone among the resources available on the Web (contents, services, people, devices, etc.), through the creation of ontologies and taxonomies that facilitate tagging and retrieval of information and knowledge, and favour automatic reasoning of intelligent agents, so creating a sort of collaboration among human beings and machines.

- *Virtual Reality Layer*: focused on shaping and creating a robust service infrastructure to offering, on multiple devices, an immersive experience based on the convergence of text, image, 3D graphics, audio and video.
- *Security and Trust Layer*: focused on shaping and creating a trustworthy infrastructure, with methods, procedure, tools and technologies that can manage privacy issues.
- *Digital Networks Layer*: focused on shaping and creating a reliable "network of networks" that can support mobile and interoperable devices, customized services and applications, heterogeneous contents and multiple delivery modes.

Figure 6.3 provides an overall vision of the Future Internet based educational framework, that can definitively enable multiple scenarios in which individuals and networks of people (with embedded and heterogeneous devices and tools, and more in general "things" that can interact with them and with other things), can access to intelligent, pervasive and fast digital networks for interacting with other people and with interdisciplinary knowledge sources and learning bases (in multimedia and multi-language formats). A set of personalized and interactive services, enhanced by semantic features, facilitate people communication, allowing them to interact effectively and securely with the applicative contexts and real life situation. 3D navigation and virtual reality tools contribute to enrich user experience and to create highly immersive environments.

The above briefly described scenarios can be interpreted as an expression of the *"informal learning"* paradigm that reveals to be more effective in a time-to-

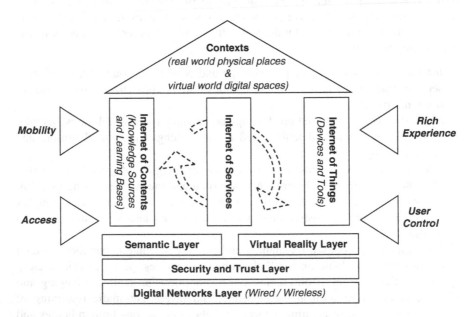

Fig. 6.3 An overall vision of the Future Internet based educational framework

performance analysis, as observed by Sally Moore at Digital Equipment Corporation (Moore 1998).

Actually, informal learning represents an "always-on" process, carried out day by day; usually it is not intentional, structured and deeply organized. It represents a comprehensive process that embraces four complementary dimensions (DIUS 2009):

- *Learning to know*: focused mainly on discovering, exploring and acquiring knowledge;
- *Learning to do*: focused mainly on developing and acquiring skills, competencies and practical abilities;
- *Learning to live together*: focused mainly on developing attitudes towards tolerance, diversity and mutual understanding;
- *Learning to be*: focused mainly on developing individual and collective personality, autonomy and mental capacity.

An emerging technological, organizational and cultural archetype that integrates formal learning and valorises informal learning approaches is the *Personal Learning Environment* (PLE).

PLEs embed the key principles of the constructivism and connectivism learning approaches:

- Learning as active and personal driven process;
- Learning as collaborative based result;
- Learning as context-based experience;
- Learning as ICT-enabled and network based practice.

PLEs stimulate also learners to develop self learning capacity, in order to create the right mindset and motivation that are at the basis of the *lifelong learning*.

The PLE concept was introduced by Olivier and Liber in 2001 (Olivier and Liber 2001), who tried to image new architectures for e-learning overcoming some limitations of the traditional learning environments and evolving them towards four main directions: (1) decentralized control and peer infrastructures; (2) interoperability among different platforms, (3) focus on functionalities, (4) support to user mobility.

After the contribution of Olivier and Liber, many other scholars analysed and studied the PLE concept.

Recently, George Siemens conceived the PLEs as decentralized models for no-sequential learning design and deployment, obtained from a collage of interoperable and integrated tools serving a particular function in the learning process (Siemens 2006).

Terry Anderson defined a PLE as a unique interface into the owners' digital environment. It integrates their personal and professional interests (including their formal and informal learning), connecting these via a series of syndicated and distributed feeds (Anderson 2006). The author developed also the concept of Personal Work and Learning Environments (P-WLE) instead of PLE, to show that learning and work are not separate areas, and that in fact learning goes on through life.

According to Wikipedia, PLEs are systems that help learners take control of and manage their own learning. This includes providing support for learners to set their own learning goals, to manage their learning content and process, to communicate with others in the process of learning, and thereby achieve their personal learning goals.

Definitively, a PLE can be considered an Internet-based framework, incorporating tools and services chosen by the learner for gathering and processing information, for creating communities and networks of people, for creating new knowledge, for developing new competencies, skills and attitudes according to dynamic, personalized and adaptive learning patterns. This framework is open to external environments, technological platforms and knowledge sources, to enrich the quality of the entire learning process. Finally, the PLE is continuously monitored and managed by a set of semi-automatic tools that suggest new patterns, new contents, new services and new people and communities that can make more effective the overall learning experience (Torres Kompen and Mobbs 2008).

Figure 6.4 shows a general PLE architecture, conceived as a loose collection, a mash-up of systems, tools, services, people and resources, as a way of harnessing the power of the network, exploiting the available standards for interoperability and integration. The configuration of a PLE ensures and promotes autonomy, encourages diversity, enables interaction and supports openness, in a networked based environment, fostering collaboration, cooperation and competence development.

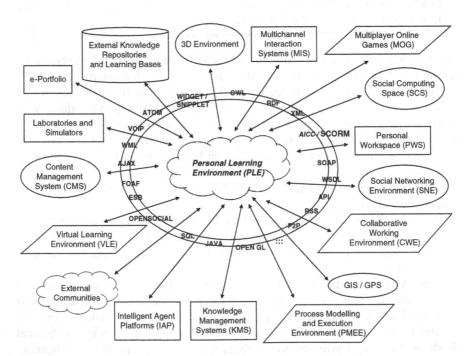

Fig. 6.4 A general PLE architecture

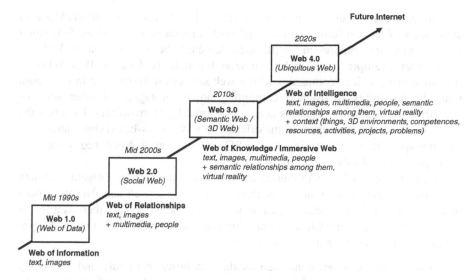

Fig. 6.5 Future evolution of the Internet

This meta-configuration and conceptualization of a PLE opens the boundaries for imagining the future evolution of the Internet along a never-end dimension, currently characterized by four main milestones represented in Fig. 6.5.

An innovative way to instance the above framework of PLE in a Web 3.0 or 4.0 scenarios is the *Cloud Computing* model.

According to this interpretation, the term Cloud Computing was initially introduced by the Google CEO Eric Schmidt, in 2006, who said: "... *It starts with the premise that the data services and architecture should be on servers. We call it cloud computing – they should be in a 'cloud' somewhere. And that if you have the right kind of browser or the right kind of access, it doesn't matter whether you have a PC or a Mac or a mobile phone or a BlackBerry or what have you – or new devices still to be developed – you can get access to the cloud ...*".

The paradigm of cloud computing introduces a hybrid model to use and exploit technological infrastructures and resources (hardware, computing power, operative systems, storage, data, applications and services), basing on the concept of scalability over the Internet. This model is based on a distributed organization of these resources on a network of interoperable clouds, operating on a world-wide dimension. The logic of usage shifts from a product-based view towards a service-based view; the only condition for end user is represented by the availability of a secure and fast wireless/wired network, a trusted access, a set of portable devices for accessing to the "clouds".

Some precursors of Cloud Computing model can be considered *Zoho.com* (that allows users to create, review, store and share slides and presentations, documents, spreadsheets, databases and other applications) or *GoogleApps* (that provides a wide range of online services to create, review, store and share documents, presentations, chat, work groups, calendars, personalized web sites, spreadsheets, for communication and collaboration). Also Microsoft is investing a lot in the cloud computing field; some examples are *Skydrive* for data storage, *FolderShare* to synchronize files and folders among different computers and systems, *Silverlight* for managing and compressing multimedia content to be delivered on the Web.

Another example is given by Amazon through its *Amazon Web Services* initiative that provides companies with a web services infrastructure in the cloud, with the possibility to use/rent computing power, storage, and other services according to the specific business demands. Similarly, Microsoft has launched the *Azure* initiative that is focused on the offering of a Windows-based environment for running applications and storing data, a SQL data server, a .Net based framework for deploying applications and running businesses.

The adoption of Cloud Computing model implies the facing of several complex challenges, mainly due to the innovativeness of the approach and the interdependence of the connected technological issues. From the other side, there is a list of potential advantages that Cloud Computing can give to individual users and organizations, such as (Kraan and Yuan 2009):

- *Flexible configuration*: conceived as the capability to rapidly and elastically scale-up and scale-down the technological – service – data configuration of the final system;
- *Ubiquity access*: that represents the capability to have the resources always available over the network, and accessible through heterogeneous and interoperable devices;
- *On-demand self-service*: that is the individual capability of end user to choose among the clouds, the most suitable configuration of data, services and computing resources according to the instantaneous demand and needs;
- *Space independence*: The provider's computing resources are usually pooled to serve all consumers using a multi-tenant model, with different physical and virtual resources dynamically assigned and reassigned according to consumer demand;
- *Pay per use*: a fee-for-service strategy is at the basis of the Cloud Computing business model, in order to promote resources' optimisation.

Referring to the logical models on the basis of the Cloud Computing, Fig. 6.6 illustrates three different kinds (Chappell 2008):

- *Software as a Service (SaaS)*: a model that is based on applications running completely in the cloud. Users usually adopt a browser or a simple client to access to the hosted applications and perform their tasks.
- *Attached Services*: a model that is based on the availability of local rich applications, whose functionalities and services can be extended and enhanced by accessing to specific services provided in the cloud.
- *Cloud Platforms*: a model that is based on the capabilities of developers to design, implement and deploy new applications and services based on the cloud platform and frameworks.

The choice of one of the above illustrated models depends mostly on the industry in which the organization acts, on the availability of suitable clouds of resources that are interesting for the organization and, finally, on the maturity level of ICT adoption, penetration and strategic use.

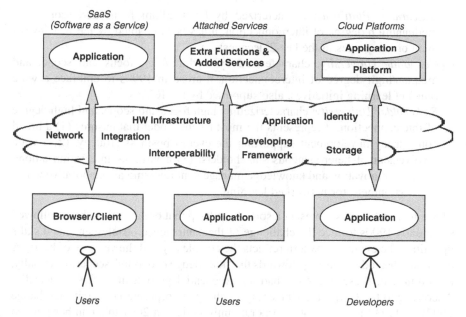

Fig. 6.6 Cloud computing models

3 Organization-Related Trends

The concept of "value" is not only referred to shareholders but it impacts mainly on stakeholders perspective (enlarging its meaning from a pure financial focus to a wider social and relational impact); accordingly, the learning process more and more involves external key actors with which organizations design, delivery, and monitor competency development initiatives.

Before introducing a possible classification of the learning initiative archetypes, we introduce three main variables that are at the basis of this classification. In detail, we are referring to the *focus*, the *scope* and the *interconnection* (Margherita and Secundo 2009).

The *focus* gives information about the training purpose (from developing specific skills to a wider set of competencies and capabilities); the *scope* provides details in terms of the involved target (from a small group of internal employees to a wider group of representatives of customers, suppliers, partners and employees); the *interconnection* gives information about the frequency and the intensity of the interactions among involved people.

According to these three parameters, it is possible to introduce the following four archetypes of learning initiatives (Margherita and Secundo 2009):

– *Training Departments*: characterized by low focus and scope, and low degree of interconnection, it expresses the nineteenth century approach of corporate education;

- *E-Learning Platforms*: characterized by low/medium focus and scope, and medium/high degree of interconnection, it has been enabled by the ICT investment of companies in the last 2 decades;
- *Corporate University*: characterized by medium/high focus and scope, and medium/high degree of interconnection, it arose in 1990s to embrace a wide range of learning initiatives, also supported by the ICT;
- *Stakeholder University*: characterized by high focus and scope, and high degree of interconnection, it represents the most recent model that ensures (1) a broad competency development supporting the overall business strategy, (2) a wide involvement of heterogeneous stakeholders, (3) a virtuous integration among research, innovation and knowledge management realizing a collaborative working environment for networked learning.

These four archetypes represent a sort of roadmap that organizations have followed since early 1900s to face the challenge of the competence obsolescence and skills updating. The evolution pattern reflects the complexity and the velocity of business dynamics that today converge towards the "knowledge economy" scenario. Actually, the number of these initiatives had an exponential growth in the last 2 decades. According to the Corporate University Exchange (Corporate University Exchange 2007), in 1993 there were 400 corporate universities; in 2001 this number jumped to 2,000; by 2010 the number will overcome 3,700 units.

Table 6.5 illustrates the different stages and models characterizing the corporate education.

Aligned with this evolution, Table 6.6 lists the main factors and trends underpinning the Stakeholder University model.

In the education field, the new organizational archetype of the "Stakeholder University" reflects today's organizations' archetype; it reveals a highly interconnected model with many heterogeneous partners and stakeholders (Clippinger 1999). The organizational boundaries are increasingly blurred, since their processes go

Table 6.5 Stages and models characterizing the corporate education

Stage/model	Training departments (1920s–1970s)	e-Learning platforms and corporate universities (1970s–1990s)	Stakeholder university (1990s–...)
Focus	Individual competencies	Organizational change	Stakeholder value
Link with strategy	Indirect	Direct	Proactive
Scope	Individual	Organization	Network of stakeholders
ICT use	PC	Intranet and Internet, web-learning, multimedia	Collaborative learning, social computing, 3d environments, simulations and games
Curricula	Business topics and functions	Leadership and workplace skills	Projects, problems, processes
Example	Disney	Toyota	Motorola

Table 6.6 Main factors and trends underpinning the Stakeholder University model

Dimension	Factor/trend
Focus	Maximum alignment between business goals and learning goals
	Integration of organizational development and research
	Integration of knowledge management and learning
	Stakeholder value as ultimate purpose
	Importance of stakeholder satisfaction and service
Scope	Network of stakeholders is the target
	Global reach and multi-localization
	Synergies with academic and industry partners
Interconnection (and ICT use)	Collaborative learning, research and innovation processes
	ICT for managing content, competencies and communities
	Social computing, open source and Web 2.0 applications
	Semantic Web, 3D and immersive reality, simulations and games
Curricula (Design and Delivery)	Holistic curricula
	Relevance of soft skills beside workplace competencies
	Business processes driving curricula design
	Integrated rather than functional/specialist knowledge
	Hands-on, action and on-demand learning approaches
Organization (and Development)	Separate entity respect to the HR function
	Strategic and operational link with the business level
	Top management fundamental for initial sponsorship
	Bottom-line support requisite for the growth of the initiative
	Personal development objectives overcome money rewards
Performance	Centrality of job outcomes and work performance
	Personal development and career growth
	Measurable impact on talent retention, productivity, capacity, efficiency and managing demographics

through different organizations belonging to different stages of the value system. New principles like *self-organization, fitness* and *co-evolution* inspire the new organization, conceived as complex adaptive systems (Clippinger 1999; Coleman 1999). The complexity of the resulting scenario cannot be controlled, as it is a dynamic and no-linear reality, but it must be managed, so the organization can benefit from it through "sense & respond" and "engage & collaborate" strategies (Tapscott 2006).

Definitively, the "Stakeholder University" can be interpreted as a concrete instance of the model into the education field, a sort of *"Learning Organization for Learning Sector"*. Actually, the original definition of Learning Organization given by Peter Senge states that *"... a learning organization is an organization where people continually expand their capacity to create the results they truly desire, where new and expansive patterns of thinking are nurtured, where collective aspiration is set free and where people are continually learning how to learn together ..."* (Senge 2000).

Applying this definition to the learning and education sector makes possible: (1) a concrete link between learning process and results, that gives the value-based perspective to the competency development programs; (2) the exploration of new patterns and ideas that can open and generate new sources of value; (3) a community-based interaction and a process-based dynamic; (4) the development of "learning to learning" skills that make possible the sustainability of the entire learning process; (5) an effective relationship between individual expectations and organizational performance, trying to exploit personal attitudes and interests, promoting distributed leadership approach, empowerment and self-organizing mechanisms.

The Stakeholder University model could be an effective answer to the critical human resources challenges identified by the BCG (Boston Consulting Group) and the EAPM (European Association for Personal Management) in the report entitled "The Future of HR in Europe – Key Challenges Through 2015" and published in 2007 (BCG and EAPM 2007). Moving from the consideration that human resources have never played a fundamental role in business than they do today, becoming so the major source of competitive advantage, this report identifies the 17 critical challenges that HR top managers have to face today for guaranteeing future sustainability and wealth of their companies.

The report has been realized through a survey involving 1,355 executives from 27 European countries, complemented by over 100 follow-up interviews to senior executives.

The results of the report help organizations and HR executives to design a medium-long term strategy for their human resources, opportunely framed in the overall social and business context characterized by the fact that:

- The fortunes of companies are built on the ideas and ingenuity of people;
- New and productive sources of labor are emerging globally, obliging so companies to hire talented people able to create value from these sources;
- Society is aging and companies are not adequately equipped to face this phenomenon;
- New industries, hiring demands and career trajectories emerge suddenly, and workers are not well prepared to live these pervasive and rapid transformations;
- Uncertainty balances the economic opportunities, and the relationship between work and life is more difficult to maintain.

In this context, organizations try to implement change, aligning and renewing their strategy, culture and model, as well as to manage the draw-back effects in their employees.

The results of the survey can be plotted in a graph as the one shown in Fig. 6.7, in which the 17 critical challenges for HR top managers are grouped in three categories, according to the degree of current capability of the HR top managers to face them and to level of future importance these challenges will have in the next years:

- High importance challenges, that are: *managing talents, managing change and cultural transformation, managing demographics, managing work-life balance, becoming a learning organization*;

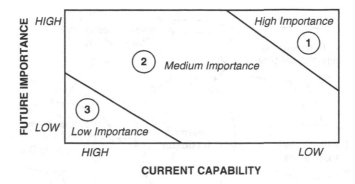

Fig. 6.7 The 17 critical challenges for HR

- Medium importance challenges, that are: *improving leadership development, transforming HR into a strategic partner, improving performance management and rewards, enhancing employee commitment, managing globalization, measuring HR and employee performance, managing diversity, managing corporate social responsibility, providing shared services and outsourcing HR*;
- Low importance challenges, that are: *delivering on recruiting and staffing, restructuring the organization, mastering HR processes.*

4 Discussion and Conclusions

Normally, "conclusion" is a word that indicates the end of a cycle, of a product, process or phase, or of a journey. In this case, we would like to consider this word as an opportunity to reflect, individually and collectively.

This phase prepares a new adventure: the implementation of the Learning Incubator model, largely, to designing and offering open and networked i-Learning experiences, involving teachers, mentors, experts, employees, public decision makers, students, managers and executives. We would like to invite readers, learning experts, human resources managers to "incubate" these initiatives according to the Learning Incubator model and its main strategic dimensions, as illustrated in Fig. 6.8:

- Involvement of heterogeneous stakeholders;
- Cross disciplinary knowledge sources and learning bases;
- Usage of knowledge sharing practices among the participants;
- Use of contextualized approaches;
- Integration and interoperability among the technological systems;
- Balance among individual, collaborative and cooperative working.

The "incubation" phase is a very delicate process for learning designers and educators. Actually, very recently, Gilly Salmon, director of the Beyond Distance Research Alliance of the University of Leicester and one of the main expert in the

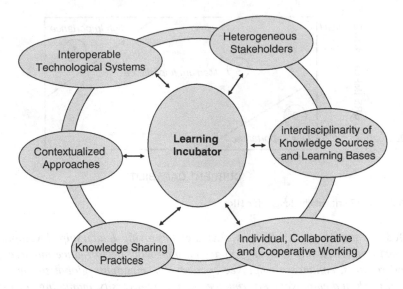

Fig. 6.8 The Learning Incubator model and its main strategic dimensions

field of e-learning research, in the occasion of the annual conference EDEN 2009 on "Innovation in Learning Communities" held in Gdansk (Poland), she affirmed that *"this is the best of times and the worst of times for open learning"*.

Actually, it is the best of times, because today's generation of educators has the tools, the techniques and the vision and it can make profit of all these potentialities. At the same time, it is also the worst one, because everything can end in a desolate flop, if today's generation of educators does not take and exploit correctly the chances it has in front.

So, it is not acceptable to be the victims of own misleading statements like *"the content is the king"* or *"everything you need for learning is in one box"*, and *"build it and they will come"* or *"academics are resistant"*, and so on. It's fundamental to foreshadow, to directly or indirectly cause a prophecy to become true, so demonstrating that a good hypothesis of work can become a successful one.

Pursuing this mission implies facing the following challenges (NESTA 2009; Van't Hooft 2008), impacting on the main actors of the learning process:

- *Learners*, who have to take responsibility for, and ownership and control of their own learning and achievements, through the adoption of a practical vision of learning process, so aiming at creating concrete products and artifacts;
- *Teachers/mentors*, whose profile is the result of the integration of multiple profiles, like the subject matter expert, the learning designer, the mentor/coacher and the learner, as well;
- *Curricula structure*, that must combine valuable knowledge with strategic skills and key attitudes, so promoting deep, inquiry-based and practical learning;
- *Partners/stakeholders*, who must inspire and motivate learners, and participate in collaborative learning design, delivery and assessment;

– *Laboratories/incubators*, conceived as new learning environments enabling innovative learning processes, also through the usage of advanced technological infrastructures and services promoting collaborative and cooperative working, formal and informal learning, with the respect of privacy, security and authenticity issues.

References

Anderson T (2006) PLE's versus LMS: Are PLEs ready for Prime time? http://terrya.edublogs. org/2006/01/09/ples-versus-lms-are-ples-ready-for-prime-time Accessed 3 January 2010

BBC (2008) Technologies on the rise in 2008. http://news.bbc.co.uk/2/hi/technology/7147804.stm Accessed 12 January 2010

BCG (Boston Consulting Group) and EAPM (European Association for Personnel Management) (2007) The Future of HR in Europe – Key Challenges Through 2015, Boston, USA

Chappell D (2008) A short introduction to cloud platforms – an enterprise oriented view, Chappell & Associates. http://www.davidchappell.com/CloudPlatforms--Chappell.pdf Accessed 29 December 2009

Clippinger J H (1999) The Biology of Business: Decoding the Natural Laws of Enterprise. Jossey Bass Publishers. San Francisco

Corporate University Exchange (2007) Six Annual Benchmarking Report

Coleman D (1999) Groupware: Collaboration and Knowledge Sharing. In: Liebowitz J (eds) Knowledge Management Handbook. CRC Press. New York

DIUS – Department for Innovation, Universities and Skills in UK (2009) The learning revolution. http://www.dius.gov.uk/skills/engaging_learners/informal_adult_learning/~/media/ publications/I./learning_revolution Accessed 5 January 2010

Economist Intelligence Unit (2008) The future of higher education: how technology will shape learning. http://www.nmc.org/pdf/Future-of-Higher-Ed-(NMC).pdf Accessed 29 December 2009

European Commission (2008) The future of the internet. ftp://ftp.cordis.europa.eu/pub/fp7/ict/ docs/ch1-g848-280-future-internet_en.pdf Accessed 16 January 2010

European Commission (2008) The use of ICT to support innovation and lifelong learning for all – A report on progress (09/10/2008). http://ec.europa.eu/education/lifelong-learning- programme/doc/sec2629.pdf Accessed 19 January 2010

Gartner (2008a) Gartner's top 10 disruptive technologies 2008-2012. http://www.gartner.com/it/ page.jsp?id=681107 Accessed 12 January 2010

Gartner (2008b) Understanding hype cycles. http://www.gartner.com/pages/story.php. id.8795.s.8.jsp Accessed 9 January 2010

Gartner (2009a) Gartner identifies the top 10 strategic technologies for 2010. http://www.gartner. com/it/page.jsp?id=1210613 Accessed 12 January 2010

Gartner (2009b) Hype cycle for education (Industry Research – ID Number G00168224)

Jones A and Issroff K (2007) Motivation and mobile devices: exploring the role of appropriation and coping strategies. ALT-J: Research in Learning Technology, 15(3): 247–258

Kirriemuir J (2008) A Spring 2008 "Snapshot" of UK higher and further education developments in second life. Eduserv virtual world watch. http://www.scribd.com/doc/7063700/ A-Spring-2008-Snapshot-of-UK-Higher-and-Further-Education-Developments-in-Second- Life Accessed 19 January 2010

Kraan W and Yuan L (2009) Cloud computing in institutions, JISC CETIS Cloud Computing Working Group. http://docs.google.com/View?id=dgssm42h_13gm33jfdg Accessed 29 December 2009

Laurillard D (2007) Pedagogical forms for mobile learning. In: Pachler N (ed) Mobile Learning: Towards a Research Agenda. Institute of Education University of London, London

Margherita A and Secundo G (2009) The Emergence of the Stakeholder University. In: Open
    Business Innovation Leadership. The Emergence of the Stake-holder University. Palgrave
    Macmillan, New York
Moore S A (1998) Time-to-Learning, Digital Equipment Corporation
NAE – National Academy of Engineering (2008) Grand challenges for engineering. http://www.
    engineeringchallenges.org Accessed 26 July 2009
NESTA – National Endowment for Science Technology and the Arts (2009), "Learning about
    Learning", Harris Federation of South London Schools, London
Olivier B and Liber O (2001) Lifelong learning: The need for portable personal learning environ-
    ments and supporting interoperability standards. http://wiki.cetis.ac.uk/uploads/6/67/
    Olivierandliber2001.doc Accessed 5 January 2010
Salmon G and Edrisinga P (2008) Podcasting for Learning in Universities. Ed. Mc Graw Hill, New
    York
Senge P (2000) Reflection on a Leader's New Work: Building Learning Organizations. In: Morey
    D, Maybury M and Thuraisingham B (eds.) Knowledge Management: Classic and Contemporary
    Works. The MIT Press, Boston
Siemens G (2006) Learning or management system? A review of learning management system
    reviews, Learning Technologies Centre at University of Manitoba, Canada
Tapscott D (2006). Winning with the Enterprise 2.0. New Paradigm Learning Corporation.
Torres Kompen R and Mobbs R (2008) Building Web 2.0-based personal learning environments – A
    conceptual framework. https://lra.le.ac.uk/bitstream/2381/4398/1/EDEN%20ResWksp%20
    2008%20Torres%20Kompen%20et%20al%20Web%202.0%20PLE%20paper.pdf Accessed
    17 December 2009
Van't Hooft M (2008) Mobile, wireless, connected, Information clouds and learning. In: Emerging
    Technologies for Learning, British Educational Communications and Technology Agency
    (BECTA). http://partners.becta.org.uk/upload-dir/downloads/page_documents/research/
    emerging_technologies08-2.pdf Accessed 15 January 2010
Volkmann C, Wilson K E, Mariotti S, Rabuzzi D, Vyakarnam S and Sepulveda A (2009)
    Educating the next wave of Entrepreneurs. World Economic Forum. http://www.weforum.org/
    pdf/GEI/2009/Entrepreneurship_Education_Report.pdf Accessed 11 December 2009
Warburton S (2009) Second life in higher education: assessing the potential for and the barriers to
    deploying virtual worlds in learning and teaching, British Journal of Educational Technology,
    40(3):414–426